A New "Normal" Now

by

Joanne D.

authorHOUSE®

AuthorHouse™
1663 Liberty Drive, Suite 200
Bloomington, IN 47403
www.authorhouse.com
Phone: 1-800-839-8640

This book is a work of non-fiction. Unless otherwise noted, the
author and the publisher make no explicit guarantees as to the
accuracy of the information contained in this book and in some

First published by AuthorHouse 10/8/2007

ISBN: 978-1-4343-2372-9 (sc)

Printed in the United States of America
Bloomington, Indiana

This book is printed on acid-free paper.

Cover quote – Alcoholics Anonymous World Services, Inc., New York, New York,
1981, page 152.

Cover quote reprinted with permission with following disclaimer:
  "The excerpt from the book, Alcoholics Anonymous reprinted with permission
  of Alcoholics Anonymous World Services, Inc. (AAWS). Permission to
  reprint this excerpt does not mean that AAWS has reviewed or approved
  the contents of this publication, or that AAWS necessarily agrees with the
  views expressed herein. A.A. is a program of recovery from alcoholism only
  – use of this excerpt in connection with programs and activities which are
  patterned after A.A., but which address other problems, or in any other non
  A.A. context, does not imply otherwise."

*This book is dedicated to all people who are suffering
through the disease of
drug addiction,
directly or indirectly.*

God bless you.

Contents

A New "Normal" Now

A Family's Journey through Drug Addiction and Recovery

Do you think there is anything on Earth worse than your own child's sudden death? Maybe watching your child die from a life threatening illness is worse, or being murdered. I think watching your child self destruct, die a self-inflicted, long suffering death on drugs is worse than anything I can think of. I know the saying "where there is life there is hope." And with death, there is no hope of a future on Earth, but for the longest time I wrestled with God to please stop the pain and hopelessness of drug addiction in my children at all costs. The pervasive thought that my child was going to die and go to hell for the sins being committed on drugs was worse than the thought of an instantaneous or even prolonged death from a "respectable" disease. I have since met many parents whose children are addicted, homeless, in mental institutions or in prison and their pain runs so deep. When all you do is pray for the healing and health of your children and receive crime (in your own home) and hurt, how do you reconcile this?

Luckily, there is a way out and many have found it before me, but few stick around to tell their stories.

My children have been sober for over 6 years and I'm **not** having a very difficult time forgetting, forgiving, and moving forward with my life. I have come to terms with my past and present and feel hopeful and enthusiastic about the future. I have a strong desire to tell my story from start to finish - partly because I want to help others and partly to lie the past to rest.

The story you are about to read is all true, except some of the names. The dates, events, time and places are all facts.

I had written this whole story using our real names. The more I thought about what might happen in the future if the truth of my children's past were known, made me decide to leave this story semi-anonymous. I realized that my intention of somehow erasing the stigma attached to drug abuse/addiction was what compelled me to change our names. I can not take the chance of erasing the stigma with my children and grandchildren's future at stake. Even if people change their lives and are productive, honest and loving members of society, others will not always forgive and trust them.

We are the family next door. We look like anybody else. Currently everyone is employed, active in church, sports, and social activities. You would never guess what we had gone through individually, and as a family. My kids are in remission. They are a drink away from the disease of alcoholism or addiction and have been for over 7 years.

My advice to families affected by drugs and alcohol is to get help for yourself. Go for your loved one but stay for yourself. You too can have the best years of your life ahead of you.

Ten years ago when drug abuse was affecting my daughter and therefore my family, I never imagined that today, I would be using that nightmarish time to help and encourage others. Not so long ago our house was full – of people, of noise, and of pain. All the children are grown-up and independent now. They have all grown in years and most importantly, they and my husband and I have grown emotionally, mentally and spiritually. We get together almost every Sunday afternoon as a family. All week long the seven of us plus spouses and grandchildren talk and share ourselves with each other. I had prayed so hard for sober children. That's all, sober children. For a long time that didn't happen.

So I developed an intense, intimate relationship with God. I put one foot in front of the other every day for many years and asked God to lead me. I followed as best I could. Then one day it happened – I realized along with this awesome relationship with God came a relationship with each and every child. I got way more than I asked for or even hoped for. That is a long stretch from a family afflicted with Drug Addiction, Obsessive Compulsive Disorder (OCD), Depression and Post Traumatic Stress Disorder (PTSD). We could very well be not speaking to one another now, never mind living near one another and sharing our spiritual growth with one another as we do today. As I am writing this tonight, Chris, my middle son, will be coming over to lead Eric (my husband), Theresa (my daughter) and I in a bible study.

I have been counseling families affected by drug abuse for over 6 years and I tell bits and pieces of my story to others. I tell how I survived drug addiction and a mental disorder in our children, codependence, memories of sexual abuse, and Post Traumatic Stress Disorder in myself - all coinciding at the same time.

In listening to so many family members share what they are going through, I realized there is so much that we all have in common. One of the most important commonalities is the desire to help our loved one get sober and then realizing we are powerless to make it happen. Sharing our stories with one another, especially what works, is one of the greatest gifts we can pass on to others.

I have written about my journey as a parent of two teenage drug addicts and all the issues that surfaced during those years. My family has graciously given permission to have some of their story told, though their names are changed. As my story unfolds I do not know my children are addicts until I get my daughter into inpatient treatment. Our lives before drug use were like a Norman Rockwell painting.

I. Our Family History:

Dating, Marriage and Children
1970 - 1995

Our family was a typical American military family, maybe even just a little bit better, at least in my eyes, because as a couple, my husband and I were after the same goals of a happy and peaceful family life. My husband, Eric, had graduated from the military academy at West Point and I had met him at a dance there. I was a young high school girl. It was August 1970, just before my senior year. I had some very good girlfriends and one of them had a brother who went to West Point. My friends and I lived about a 40 minute drive from there and one time we all decided to spend the weekend away, well a Saturday night anyway. My friend's brother had told us about a dance they were

1

having at West Point and about a hotel dorm for girls where we could stay at for $3.00/night. We all decided it would be fun and we would not get involved with any one guy. We would "play the field".

We all packed up our things and hopped in my friend's car for a night away. The dance was very interesting to say the least. There were about 200 guys and 20 girls. It was a great boost for all of our egos. There was one guy who kept hitting on us all. At one point my friend and I were hiding in the bathroom from this guy and we were going to make a mad dash across the dance floor to the other side. (This was our idea of letting a guy down gently!) As we crossed the floor a really sweet guy, Eric, stopped me and asked me to dance. I said yes and the rest, as they say, is history.

I didn't keep my promise about *not* staying with one person. Eric asked me if I wanted some pizza and soda and I said yes. As we sat outside on the patio overlooking the lake we just couldn't stop talking. Not only that, Eric really seemed interested in all I had to say. We met again the following morning for a canoe ride and just playing on the beach. When it was time to leave Eric wanted my phone number and my friend said he should get my address. I don't know why she insisted on my address but Eric wrote my address on the inside of a matchbook using a burned match. A letter came a few days later addressed to Red Nose Rd. instead of Red Mills Rd.! I'm glad the Post Office took a really good guess. I wrote back and we started talking on the phone.

Eric and I dated for three years. I graduated high school and Eric was there. I went to Nursing School for two years. My family made a drastic move from New York to Indiana because of my dad's job. I stayed at college in New York for my second semester and my parents even left me the second car so I could visit Eric and just get around if I needed to. For the third and fourth semesters I moved out to Indiana with my family. I missed them so much and I found it too difficult to concentrate on my studies. Eric and I would try to visit one weekend a month and for holidays. He was the nicest man I had ever met and I loved being with him. We married as soon as we could which was right after his graduation in June of 1973. I graduated from college two months later in August as a Registered Nurse with an Associates Degree.

We had our first baby, William, the year after we were married. The following year we had Ann; two years later, Christopher; and two and a half years later, Theresa; and in another two years Michael. I kept up my Nursing license thinking someday, when the children were older, I would go back to work. And after our tour in Germany in 1984, I took an RN refresher course and worked part time for a doctor during the evening and weekend hours. Our youngest child, Michael was almost four years old, our oldest son, William, was 11 and I felt like I was able to leave the kids for two evenings a week and every other Saturday. Eric was usually home and if he wasn't, I hired a babysitter.

After 4 years in Aberdeen, MD we moved to Pittsburgh and I worked again part time for a doctor. I did this for another 3 years. In 1991, when our three older kids were in high school and our younger two were in middle school we moved back to Maryland. William, our oldest son, was very anxious about this and seemed to have more anger than usual. We were living in the country in Howard County, Maryland and in order to get anywhere the kids needed rides. I thought putting off working outside the home for a few more years would benefit everyone. So I stayed at home and did some volunteer work at the schools and church.

William was a very active child and was diagnosed with Attention Deficit Disorder (ADD) in the fifth grade. We did not tell him this because we thought he would use this diagnosis as an excuse to keep doing poorly in school. We held him back that year, blaming his broken leg the year before as the reason for "not catching up." As he got older and ready to graduate high school, he seemed to become a lot more responsible. He was looking into the community college and working as a cashier at a local grocery store. He was a dedicated wrestler on the high school wrestling team. Ann had always been an excellent student and a responsible person. She was in the National Honor Society, helped me with teaching Sunday school, and earned money by babysitting in the neighborhood. Her goal was to attend a college with a good reputation. She wanted to live away from home and have that "real" college experience. Chris was following William in his wrestling program and Ann in her scholastic record. He seemed to enjoy a well-rounded social life a little more than the other two. He was very kind and sensitive. Theresa seemed to have it all. In Middle School, her attitude was fun and loving, her grades were above average, and she had great athletic abilities. In the eighth grade she was one of two girls who made the dance team for high school. Michael had about the same personality except he did not have the grades or the desire for the grades. He did a minimal amount of schoolwork, raised a lamb for the 4-H, played goalie for the soccer team and just got along well with his buddies.

Eric's job was very time consuming. He was a Lieutenant Colonel working at a research facility in Bethesda, MD. This was a very high pressure and stressful time in his life and I really felt like I needed to support him by staying at home and being there for him and the kids. I must be honest and say it was a hard decision either way: to stay home with the kids or to work outside the home.

As for our marriage, we struggled to make time for each other. It seemed that in a short time I would be able to cut all the apron strings with the kids and get out in the world on my own. I thought of going back to college for a teaching degree. I loved working and being with children and my own were growing up. Eric and I were talking about retirement after 20 years in the Army. He was looking into teaching jobs for himself at some local colleges. We loved our house in Howard County on one acre of land. This was going to be the home we would retire in. We looked forward to that empty nest syndrome everyone talks about.

II. Noticing Changes

In the summer of 1994, just before Theresa entered the ninth grade she had made the High School Drill and Dance Team. It was quite an honor and she did look beautiful when she danced. I thought she looked as if that was what she meant to do. She seemed to come alive and as she danced you could feel the joy.

However, this was around the time I noticed the change in her personality. I knew something was different right away because *our* relationship changed. Theresa would go right up the stairs to her room whenever she came home and she didn't talk with me like she used to. I could see that her friends were changing along with her appearance, her neatness and her attitude. I was concerned and I didn't like it but it wasn't offensive – yet.

The first real scare for me came when Theresa and Michael were supposed to be in their Confraternity of Christian Doctrine (CCD) classes at church one Monday night. At this time, Theresa was in the eighth grade and Michael in the seventh. I received a phone call that I needed to come down to the church. When Eric and I arrived at the church, the director of Religious Education and the police met us. We were told that a window in the church had been broken and that our kids were somehow involved. They had skipped class with two other kids and tried to put the entire blame on the other two. I say "tried" because we left the church and arrived home to find out that we had to go back because there was no doubt that our kids were just as involved as the other two and were being sent to talk to a juvenile probation officer. I'm not sure what was worse the actual event or the lying. They were given a few hours of community service (washing police cars) and they promised to stay out of trouble.

Our church offered a new kind of religion classes that involved the whole family attending together so we switched from the Monday evening classes. Theresa, Michael, Eric and I attended this family class once a month together after Mass. Then we would all go to Pizza Hut for lunch. The older boys worked and didn't go to church any more so they would meet us at Pizza Hut just before or after their jobs. Although I was a little disappointed that the boys didn't go to church, it was a pleasant time for me watching the kids start to make their way in the world and all of us coming together for a little while every Sunday for lunch. I also knew they had a firm foundation in their faith and one day they would find their way.

Then one Sunday, just after church, it must not have been a religion class day, Eric, Theresa, Michael and I arrived home and Chris told us that the police had been by to ask Theresa a few questions about a boy that was in trouble and had run away. She denied knowing anything about what had happened. She said she didn't know him that well and she didn't know why the police would be asking her questions. The next thing I heard was that he was put in a rehab center for drugs, after threatening his mother with a knife. I think right here I sensed a dramatic change in her attitude because there was no further commenting or conversation about the incident. Looking back I wish there had been some drug program I could have looked into just for guidance or even as a way of sending a stronger message to her that I was aware of her changes.

One night, right after this incident, around two in the morning I heard the back sliding glass door close very gently. I wondered who was up and went downstairs to check. The door was unlocked. We always locked the doors. So I went to check all the beds and found that Theresa was missing. I woke Eric up and the two of us went downstairs to lie down on the couch to wait for her to come home. Hours passed and finally I heard the smallest creaking on the steps and I saw Theresa. "Come and sit with us", I said. Although we attempted to communicate with her, she only commented was that she went out to meet some friends and that she was sorry. I asked if they had been drinking and I never got a straight answer, only assurances she'd never sneak out again.

I could see that my daughter was changing drastically by her isolating behavior and all the relationships in our family were becoming less fun and more work. I would plan a family day out and something would come up. Theresa would have to do something else. Usually it involved the dance team and I knew how important that was to her. I also knew, in general, teens liked to spend less time with their family. I noticed one screen was knocked out of the window in Michael's room. Whenever I put it back it would be out on the garage roof again. Also, I'd find aluminum foil or pieces of pens all around the house. The water filters would be missing from the faucets and pieces of window screens would be cut out. Whenever I asked the family about this, no one seemed to know anything about these strange occurrences.

Eric and I had been talking about retiring and settling down in Maryland. I was living in my dream home in a beautiful part of the country. Our choices were to either look for work around this area or accept orders for San Antonio. However, with all the bad things going on, we thought for Theresa's sake we would move out of the area. San Antonio had always been my least favorite place to live mostly because of the extreme heat in the summer. I nick named it "hell" because I hated living here back in 1980 when Eric was stationed here for a six month military course. We were given orders to move with 4 children under the age of 6 when one child was starting kindergarten and the other, first grade. The course Eric took kept him busy from 5:00 in the morning to late night study sessions. I left all my friends and really didn't have quite enough time to establish new friends. So basically for a few months I was on my own and then we were given orders for Germany. I was not allowed to travel with Eric until there was housing available in Germany yet I was also not allowed to stay on base in San Antonio while we waited. This time in my life was very frustrating and lonely. I ended up moving in with my parents for the few months it took Eric to find housing in Germany. I hated the whole process of moving and living in San Antonio for 6 months that I vowed I'd never return again. *Now, 15 years later, I would move anywhere to help my daughter, even "hell".*

The three oldest kids were in college, not moving with us, and they were really becoming very independent. So Eric and I accepted the orders for San Antonio and would move as soon as possible to get Theresa away from drugs and her drug using friends.

III. The Move to San Antonio

November 1995

Eric went ahead of us to San Antonio while I stayed behind to sell the house in Maryland. Our plans were to try and have the kids start their new school in the fall; however, we just had to wait. Time passed and the house wasn't selling. With three kids in college and two teenagers at home we were stretched financially to our limit and one of the things we intended to do was live in "quarters" on the Army base in San Antonio. There was a waiting list for these houses so we found the next best place we could. As usual we had done a lot of research in finding the "right" area to live in and Eric had rented a house in a good school district.

It was very sad packing up everything. I was having a difficult time watching Theresa become more and more distant. It seemed better to me to just get her away from the problems of being late for school, constantly wanting to go out with friends, and dropping grades. I thought a geographical move would help not realizing Theresa was already hooked on drugs and she would need a lot more help than just a change of school and friends. Our house didn't sell, so we hired a property manager to rent out our house in Maryland. This was in October and by November we were getting ready to go. The college kids came home for Thanksgiving and we were packing to move to San Antonio that weekend. They had no warning that this would be their last visit to the home they thought would be our permanent retirement residence. I was in such a hurry to stop the insanity of dealing with a child who seemed to be self destructing that moving became a solution.

There was a dusting of snow on the ground as we left Glenwood, Maryland. It is a picture that is etched in my mind forever. It was the beauty I loved about the home I thought we would retire in. It marked a time of closing a dream-like chapter and opening up a nightmare chapter in the life of our family.

When we arrived in San Antonio, and all through the drive down here, Theresa and Michael gave us a lot of grief for moving. I knew it would be difficult but I had a lot of hope that the change in environment would help. I also thought that if given a chance we all might be able to spend some quality time together during the trip south and start back on the right path. We had searched out the schools and found a high school with a great reputation. Within a few days after starting school Theresa came home from school in the back of a pick up truck with a load of boys. It was very scary looking and my heart sank as I realized that she was continuing with the same behavior and lifestyle, only with different people. A few weeks later it was Christmas time. William called one night from college and said Theresa was not doing well and we needed to do something. He could tell by talking to her on the phone. I could also see that things were going right back to the way they were in Maryland. Only it was worse because all the places and friends were new to all of us so it added to the stress of the unknown.

We decided to get psychiatric counseling at a child psychiatry clinic on the military base because we had no idea what to say or do. Our clinical counseling appointments consisted of Theresa going in some of the time to talk, Eric and me going in at other times and a mixture of all of these. I noticed that we talked about the same things over and over again but nothing was changing. We received no feedback or suggestions, just validating the things that we said. Meanwhile, Theresa was getting worse and we were being told at the clinic, "Yes, she does experiment with drugs but it's not that bad".

One night about 9:00 PM Theresa said she was going for a walk. I thought it was strange and I asked Eric to follow her. As he walked up the street in the direction she was headed he saw Theresa walking out of a neighbor's garage with a six pack of their beer that had been stored in the garage refrigerator. Eric had her return it and brought her home. We tried to talk and reason with her but all we got was a "non-response" response.

Sometimes Theresa would not come home right after school. She was going to try and make the high school dance team at her new school and it seemed reasonable for her to stay late. There would be times she did not make it home for dinner and then wanted to spend time alone in her room. She'd be on the phone endlessly and it seemed natural for her to be grieving for all her old friends. She was allowed to call friends in Maryland in the evening or on weekends when the rates were low. She was also trying to make friends in the new neighborhood.

We were still attending church as a family. However it was getting more difficult to get Theresa and Michael out of the house in time for Mass. They were rebelling against the idea that they had to go to church. One Sunday while Eric was away I told Theresa and Michael we were going to church. I was a little frantic because they were moving so slow. When we finally arrived at church everyone was standing for the entrance song. We took our places and I looked at Michael and Theresa. Theresa was wearing a mini-skirt, black nail polish, rolling her eyes and tapping her fingers on the pew in front of her as she chewed her gum. Michael was droopy, looking down, with baggy pants hanging around his underwear, barely able to stand up. We were late and the entrance song was being sung. I distinctly remember hearing "Many are the blessings He bears to those who trust in His ways…" I thought of how much I had trusted God. I thought that God wanted me to move, to be a good mother, to do all the right things and even go get help for my daughter. Where were my blessings? I was alone in a city I used to refer to as "hell", my older children were away at college, my husband was traveling, and these two kids were so defiant.

All of a sudden I started to cry. I ran out of church and as I passed Michael and Theresa I whispered, "I don't feel good". I cried so hard when I reached the car. I was trapped and I didn't know how to get out. I find it strange as I look back on this because when our oldest son William was 13 he was given a choice to go to church with us or not. It seemed the harder my kids wanted freedom the more I wanted control. During Mass Theresa came to check on me and she asked if I was alright. I said "No." And I proceeded to yell at her for all the things she was doing to me and the family. She just looked at me and said she was going back inside. She was now inside at Mass where I wanted to be and I was sitting in the car crying. This is where I realized the disease of addiction was affecting me but I still believed Theresa was the one needing help, not me.

As it turns out our name was moving up on the list for government housing. Eric and I would meet during his lunch break and just drive around the marching fields in the center of the base and talk. "Do you know that if our children get in trouble on a military base it could go on my record or I could get kicked off the base?" Eric was telling me. With Theresa sneaking out and getting into trouble at school it just seemed too scary. The more we talked the more we decided not to jeopardize Eric's career and we would stay in our rental on the north side of town.

A few days after Theresa's sixteenth birthday, I found a note in her room. It said "Happy Fucking Birthday to me!" It was written in blood. I was so scared about Theresa's state of mind. We were still seeing the therapist at the military base child psychiatry clinic. They talked with her and asked her to sign a contract not to hurt herself but she refused. I felt light headed, like you could knock me over with a feather. The military counselor said things like "Yes she's experimenting with drugs" or "when can you come in again?" I went numb as Eric, Theresa and I left the clinic because I wasn't sure what was happening, was there any place left to turn for help? I did not understand a thing about drug addiction, and wasn't even sure that was what we were dealing with because I seemed to be the only person seeing the need for help for addiction and the "professionals" were just going along with me finding a drug rehab. I fluctuated in and out of denial of my daughter being a drug addict. I felt very inadequate and weak. It wasn't like me at all to not talk to people and ask the right questions, especially when the welfare of my child was at stake. I cried. I was becoming overwhelmed in this process.

I knew drugs were causing Theresa to become the depressed and withdrawn person before me and she was falling fast. I saw all the signs – the change of friends, clothes, attitude, drop in grades, loss of sleep at night, more sleep in the day, irregular eating habits and the general sloppiness and disrespect of self and others. There were no real legal or school consequences because either Theresa knew how to stay out of trouble or she was just lucky. We had already made a geographical move to change the environment and that hadn't worked. I was using the medical service as my last resource.

Not really sure where to go from here we asked the people at the psychiatric clinic for places that helped more with drug abuse. The clinic helped us find a list of treatment facilities. Eric and I were on the phone and we decided to split the list to call and find out about the different programs. After hanging up the phone with Eric, I had to call him back. All I could think of was the opening line that I needed to say; "I think my daughter is a drug addict and she needs help". My heart was broken and I knew the words would not be able to come out without a complete breakdown on my part. So I called Eric back and asked him if he wouldn't mind making all the phone calls. He said he'd do it.

A little while later he called back to tell me about the different places we could seek help. One of the places was called Palmer Drug Abuse Program (PDAP).

IV. Palmer Drug Abuse Program

(PDAP)

The news about the Palmer Drug Abuse Program was good. It was free of charge and Theresa didn't have to be hospitalized. It was something we could go to in the evenings and have counseling appointments when necessary and then they had sober, fun activities on the weekends. That seemed like an excellent place to start.

It was March of 1996 and Theresa's attitude was becoming more and more defiant. I wasn't sure how to get her to her first meeting so I just decided to tell her get in the car, that we were going out and it wouldn't be for long. I wasn't sure of the best way to handle the situation and I guess I just made it the easiest for me.

How long I would be able to "make" her go to meetings I didn't know but I did know I was losing what little relationship we had left and she needed help.

As we drove up to the PDAP building I noticed how run down and poor the old converted barrack type building appeared. The sign in front read "Palmer Drug Abuse Program Confidential and Free". There were teenagers hanging all around the building, some had spiked hair of different colors, many of them had body piercings and some of them had chains coming from parts of their bodies, others had chains coming from pockets or belts. The scariest body piercing was the one that was connected from the mouth to the ear by a chain. Many of them were smoking cigarettes (this was before it was illegal for them to smoke and it was only illegal for them to buy cigarettes). My heart sank into my stomach. Theresa was so smart and beautiful and my hopes for her were to go to college and become a very successful person. She had a very innocent look and she was soft spoken and gentle. In eighth grade she had been in the gifted and talented program. Now Eric and I were escorting her to a drug abuse program.

One of the PDAP counselors was out on the steps and she made it a point to say hello to Theresa and I really appreciated that because of the scowl that was on Theresa's face. Looking back it probably matched the look on my face also. It was a long night for me and I couldn't stop my eyes from tearing. We went to a newcomers meeting and were given a packet with all kinds of useful information. One statement that really affected my husband was that there was an 80% better chance for our daughter to get well if her family was involved, whether or not she was involved. As for me, I knew that I had to try anything because she was sinking fast. I kept hearing things like acceptance and serenity. I had no idea how this would help my child. However, they did say to make an appointment with a PDAP counselor so I had a little hope I'd find something out there. Another point they made was to get a sponsor. My husband should ask a man, I should ask a woman and Theresa should ask a girl in the group. This person would help us "work the steps" (see page 105). All I had to do was ask. The idea was if nothing new was coming in, nothing new was going out. I viewed a sponsor as sort of our own personal sounding board and mentor.

The next week we had our first counseling appointment. The PDAP counselor seemed interested in Theresa and really listened to what Eric and I said. I felt this was an improvement over what the other counselors at child psychiatry did for us. The only thing the PDAP counselor really said was for me to get a sponsor and start working the program and she would ask Theresa to do the same thing. She asked that Theresa try the program for a month and Eric and I commit to three months. It seemed like it was worth a shot and we had absolutely nothing to lose. There was a small brother and sister's group for teens that were related to drug abusers to go to also. *There is an increased risk that siblings will turn to drugs and/or alcohol too, or will be negatively affected, that help for these forgotten family members is often put off until the symptoms are critical. Currently in PDAP we have two "New Generation" groups. One group is for*

9-13 year olds and the other is for 13-18 year olds. So the very next meeting, we brought Michael with us. After the meeting we were very saddened and surprised to learn that Michael had gone to the user group with Theresa. Well, I thought at least we got it early enough with him. Spring break was coming up the next week and we had planned to be out of town visiting both our parents in Florida and going to Eric's cousin's wedding. So with a little more hope than before we set off on our vacation.

V. Spring Break

March 1996

Eric's family lives in Tampa and my parents live in Daytona Beach (in the winter). Eric, Theresa, Michael and I drove from Texas through Louisiana, Alabama, and Georgia and into Florida in two days. We arrived in Tampa, Florida at lunchtime and we decided to eat before arriving at Eric's family's house. We stopped at a fast food place and after lunch I used the bathroom right after Theresa before leaving the restaurant. The toilet wasn't finished flushing and I can't tell you in words how shocked I was to see Theresa's food from lunch in whole chunks floating in the toilet. She had made herself throw-up. On top of all the drug use, she was Bulimic.

When I got back to the table I asked her to talk to me. I asked her why she was throwing –up her food. She would only give me "I don't know, don't worry" type of answers. I tried to have a good time at Eric's family house but I really was uncomfortable. Later on when we went to the wedding I noticed that Theresa was just sitting alone at the table and she eyed only people's drinks, not the people, just their drinks. She would watch the drinks go from the person's mouth down to the table and from the table back up to their mouth. Her eyes roamed from drink to drink. I watched her watch different people raise their glasses up to their mouths and then set the glass back down. How my heart broke again seeing my daughter not care about the normal things teenagers care about, but only about alcohol. I thought of how normal 16-year-old girls like to look at boys and how the Theresa I knew loved to dance and what I was watching was very abnormal. Her internal joy about dancing and life was gone and I could see her pain.

My sister-in-law, Peggy, was also noticing this and she became very hypervigilent. Peggy got up and left our table whenever Theresa did and would follow her around. Although I knew this wasn't very healthy for Peggy, it did relieve me from worry for a little while and I actually enjoyed a few hours of "letting go".

At my parent's house in Daytona Beach, I was able to share some of what was going on with my parents. My mom was supportive and understanding that I had nothing to do with Theresa's drug and alcohol use. A comment my mother made was "At least you know you have nothing to feel guilty about, you had nothing to do with her using drugs!" She said I had done all the right things. Wow! That was quite a compliment and it was something I would remind myself of later through the whole recovery process because as time moved forward I felt more and more responsible for the addiction.

It seemed like whenever Theresa went into the bathroom I felt nervous. I believed she was either getting high or maybe throwing up. The worry started to consume me. I saw that she was becoming more and more distant and withdrawn. Eric was also seeing the same thing. We called the counselors at PDAP about what to do. They made an appointment for us to come in and talk when we got back from Florida. What a relief!

When we came back from the "vacation" I took Theresa in for her counseling appointment. The PDAP counselor asked me if I needed to talk to her first. I said yes. I had so much to tell the PDAP counselor. Theresa had been into so much and had stopped talking to us completely. I knew we were losing her and I felt so helpless. I went on a good 15 or 20 minutes just talking about all my worries. The PDAP counselor said, "I really feel sorry for you." I stopped dead in my tracks "You do? Why?" "Because you're trying to control something that you have no control over." I didn't know that.

For the next 5 minutes I cried. I didn't know I couldn't control what was going on. At one point in the session I said "You don't know how hard I've been trying to stop Theresa from doing what she was doing. I spent night and day thinking and planning all sorts of ways to help her. No one ever said I couldn't stop her. I thought drug prevention worked. It can't be in my family."

The PDAP counselor left me for a minute and then came back with a song for me to listen to. It was called "Let Me Go" by Susan Ashton. It's a song about turning a loved one over to God and letting them go to live their own life even if they die a fool's death. (I use it now as a step one meditation song). This was basically, the time I knew that God wanted me at PDAP. I didn't say it out loud but in my head I cried to God "You want me here, God?" "Here, in a drug abuse program! Not helping out in a nice comfortable church somewhere?" I could feel Him responding that this was the place I was supposed be. I didn't know why but I would follow His lead.

At the end of the session, I asked the PDAP counselor if I could take my sponsors place at the upcoming retreat since she was unable to attend. I also asked the PDAP counselor if I could ride up with her. I really didn't know anyone in the program and I didn't know my way around Texas at all. It really irritated me that they had a retreat for parents when the kids were out using drugs. Eric offered to stay home with Theresa and Michael. So I was on my way into what I later found out to be the process of recovery.

VI. My First Recovery Retreat

Spring 1996

I had so much trouble sleeping that first night. I was in the top bunk in the "mom's" cabin and I had a moonlit view of the woods and hills. I lay in bed for hours. I was using Ann's (our other daughter) quilt for my blanket and I could smell her after-bath fragrance. I never really realized how important a person's smell was until that night. I wondered how she was at college, and then I wondered how my son's, William and Chris, were at college also. Was Theresa out using tonight? How was Michael handling all of this? We had moved here only a few months ago and my life was changing so drastically. I yearned for the old days of

26

our hectic and fun times, living in the house Eric and I had thought we'd retire in after his military career.

William was in his own apartment in a "not-so-good section" of Towson, MD. My heart had ached when I left him there. The apartments we left him in for college were the best we could afford but were very cheap and I could see some scary looking people, probably drug addicts, wandering around. Chris was safe at a good Christian college except that his roommate was also a drug user. I knew Chris was strong in his resilience to say no to using drugs but my heart ached for all my children. Sleeping in a bunk in a cabin with a bunch of women I didn't know on the small chance that this might somehow give me the answers to help my drug using daughter was very humbling and humiliating and as the night wore on I became more and more depressed about where I was in life and where I had hoped to be by the time I was middle aged.

The next day of the retreat I remember hearing a speaker talk about how a mother had searched all over town for her son and some of the bizarre behavior in trying to control her son's drug using. I was surprised how bizarre it sounded as she talked, even though I had done many of the same things and even worse, to find and stop (control) the actions of my daughter. We split up into small groups and we were supposed to share something about ourselves. I had been up most of the night before, missing the college kids and feeling really sad about Theresa and wondering if I was even capable of being a parent to Michael through this ordeal. I realized I had no thoughts about my own feelings because all I knew was my daughter was out there using and I couldn't stop her. When my turn came to say something I started to cry.

"I don't know what to say about myself because I don't know where I end and Theresa begins or I begin and Theresa ends." This so horrified me that I felt paralyzed with fear and wept uncontrollably. *This is a big symptom of codependency - not knowing where you begin and someone else ends. Other symptoms are being obsessed with someone else's behavior, not taking care of oneself on all levels (emotionally, spiritually, physically, and mentally), and many more. (Any book by Melody Beattie is a great resource for Codependency.)*

The facilitator of the group said "thank you for reminding us where we came from". That too horrified me. I was one of *them* and I didn't want any part of it. I only wanted my old life back.

I was feeling pretty worthless. We had an afternoon break and I was at the river with many of the other parents. There were some ladies there with the PDAP counselor. The PDAP counselor was fishing and she offered her pole to me and told me where to cast the hook. I caught a fish. It made me laugh and I tried again. I went on to catch four more fish. In my mind after I caught the fifth fish I felt as though they represented all my children and somehow we would remain a family. It was time to go back to the meeting. This was the beginning of a hobby for me (fishing) that brought me back to happy childhood memories and my husband and me to many great times together.

I can't really say what the afternoon session was about or the evening but I do remember talking with other parents of drug users/addicts and just feeling like I was unable to cope with anything. I did my share of complaining and crying and by the time I went to bed I was feeling totally hopeless and helpless. I lay awake again smelling the sheets that had Ann's smell and looking outside at the stars. How I missed Ann and William and Chris. How could I be so unhappy and lonely? My busy and exciting family that I was part of was gone and I was afraid they were gone forever. I couldn't sleep and I went out for a walk.

I didn't intend to contemplate suicide but that's what I did. I sat on a bridge and cried and prayed. I remembered so many of the signs and symptoms of drug use that at the time I hadn't understood. The window screens removed from the window and lying on the garage roof outside the kids bedroom, the pieces of aluminum foil tightly rolled, faucets without filters, spray paint cans not being packed by the movers. Then, I remembered all the changes in behavior, appearance, friends, everything. Could I have done anything sooner? Then the most horrible war occurred in my head. I looked at the rocky dry riverbed many feet below. I felt like a bystander as the thoughts of jumping off the bridge took over. I imagined how I would jump and what if, after I had jumped and I was on my way down, I couldn't follow through and I tried to save myself. But in trying to save myself I actually lived through the fall but I was unable to use my arms and legs or worse my mind. At times the pain was so great

I could look down and think of only relief, at other times I thought of several people who I knew loved me and that I might actually really hurt them if I died. I believed one of the worst things a person could ever do is to take your own life yet there I was – it was happening to me. After agonizing over this I chose to live and decided that I had to put one foot in front of the other and just keep going a step at a time, a minute at a time. I was powerless, life was unmanageable and God was walking me through.

This was where I committed myself to the recovery process because it was all I had. I was convinced that God had sent me to San Antonio and PDAP for a reason. After this weekend I met with my sponsor as much as possible so I could get the steps done.

There are twelve steps in PDAP (see page 125) just like any other 12 twelve step program. PDAP has modified some of the steps to help teenagers. Any twelve step program has the same principals. Basically in PDAP (1) there is something wrong in my life, (2) I'll make new friends and change, (3) there is something outside me that's stronger and I'll call him God, (4) I'll let him take care of me. (5) I will do my part by cleaning house, (6) talk this over, and (7) turn it all over to God, (8) and become willing to do what is necessary, (9) and make amends. Then, (10) every day I will look at myself, (11) spend time in prayer and meditation, and (12) help others.

To me the steps seemed easy and self-explanatory and I could accept everything about them. The only thing I could not accept was that my daughter may never stop using drugs. It was a thought that haunted me. How in the world could such a beautiful and sweet girl like Theresa who came from such a good home ever stay on drugs? The inventory seemed like more work, but being raised Catholic, confession was a way of life and I knew it was good for the soul. I would do all these steps.

VII. It's A Disease

Every month or two at PDAP, there was an education night instead of a meeting. A counselor would come in and instruct the family members on different aspects of the disease of addiction. It was at one of these classes that I heard the instructor say that she (Theresa) doesn't want to be a drug addict/alcoholic. It's a disease that happened to her. She made a mistake when she used but now it's more than that. She's sick, but once she learns that she has the disease she is responsible for her recovery. Wow! That was a relief to me because for so long I didn't know what was wrong, why she couldn't just say "no". She lost that power when she said "yes" to trying drugs and became addicted. Just like any treatment for a disease it has to be followed, in order for recovery to take place.

The addiction may not have started right at the first joint, drink, or pill. (I have heard that for some people it does start right away). But it usually works its' way through stages.

The first stage or phase is the experimental stage. Many people try drugs/alcohol not all become addicts/alcoholics. Many of us older people (over 50) think of the potency of drugs like they were when we were young. They are much stronger now. In this stage the good effect of the drug is outweighing the negative consequence, if there is even any negative consequence at all.

The second stage is the learning stage. This is where there was so little negative consequence and a lot of perceived benefits that the person learns what feels the best, when it feels the best, and how often to use to feel good. If negative consequences are felt and seen by the person he/she learns that this is not the direction he wants his life to go and it causes him to quit. Social drinkers remain here (and I assume moderate pot smokers also); alcoholics and drug addicts move into the next phase.

The next phase is called the Preoccupation Phase. Loss of control is usually here because the negative consequences are outweighing the positive but the person continues to use. The disease is taking over and without intervention the person continues on into the Harmful Dependency Phase. The end result of this disease is jail, institution or death.

Joanne D.

Well no wonder parents, spouses and siblings are at their wits end when they are watching a loved one die of this disease that they can't do anything about. Or can they?

I believe entering a twelve-step program will provide the tools necessary for realizing what is helpful and what is enabling. Caretaking and enabling prevent the natural consequences from occurring and cause resentment on the part of the caretaker. So many young users think their parents are the "sick" ones because of all the anger and irrational behavior they are witnessing. I believe the 12 steps, education and interaction with other "recovering" families are the greatest benefit for coming through this disease with the best relationship with yourself, others and God. You're loved one may, or may not, get better; but you will be better, and become healthy in spirit, body, and mind. If your loved one does recover he/she will have a healthy, recovering family to be a part of.

VIII. Drug Rehabilitation (Family Roles)

May 1996

Theresa had been sober about 20 days at PDAP before she asked if she could go with a friend and her family to their lake house. Since she seemed to be doing so well we let her go with this friend over the weekend. Then, while she was away, I found a note that they communicated about their plans to use ("smoke out") over the weekend. And when I went to do the wash on Monday morning all Theresa's clothes were sitting in the washer, unwashed and full of mud.

It was painfully evident when she started getting high again. The withdrawal and isolation from the family started and I could see a general lethargic, distance in her eyes. Eric was on a TDY assignment (a military term for business travel) to Maryland and in a way it was a blessing. I could see the reality of the disease taking over Theresa's life and how hard it was for Eric to accept this. Many times during the next few years, when we disagreed on what to do, I'd have to remind myself he loved her as much as I did. Also my ideas didn't always work either. In fact, there would be times that he would say let's handle something one way and I'd say let's do it another way and then the next week we would have each switched positions.

I called the PDAP counselor and we discussed inpatient treatment. It was time to confront all this and seek more intense help. The first obstacle to overcome was getting the insurance to pay. Luckily, after many hours on the phone I was able to get the okay. *(This process has many loopholes. Since 1996 it has gone downhill and has become a lot harder to get good rehabilitation coverage for alcoholism/addictions).* The rehab facility did work with me on getting the insurance coverage and on setting things up for the next day for a smoother admittance to the facility.

The next obstacle was confronting the actual denial that is so profound in drug addiction. I couldn't just drive her to rehab without her consent (Texas law states that anyone over 16 years of age cannot be admitted without their consent). She would have to want help. What if she refused? How could I handle that? I decided to make an appointment for her at PDAP and have the counselor there help me. Theresa went to school as usual that morning and I told her I'd pick her up in a little while for the appointment. I packed her bags after she left, put them in the trunk, and I called her PDAP friend who had driven her to school so he would know not to pick her up after school. I took her for her "appointment" with so much anxiety and at the same time so much love in my heart.

During the appointment the PDAP counselor talked to Theresa about just going to look at a rehab facility and seeing if she might like it. No commitment was necessary. She had told Theresa she would never ask anything of her that she didn't already do herself. By this time I felt like I was starting to numb out. I got all the courage I could muster and asked the PDAP counselor to come with me to admit Theresa. I don't know why I didn't feel I could do it alone or why I would ask someone who was so busy with so many people who needed her, but there I was asking for help from a person who has made a difference. She said yes and I felt relief. The hour and half drive up to the rehab was strained. Theresa sat in the back seat and I imagined her wanting to jump out of the moving car. There have been stories of kids doing this.

When we arrived at rehab we met with one of the hospital counselors that worked there. She took time to talk to Theresa while the PDAP counselor and I walked around and waited and waited. After several hours they came back and said Theresa was ready to get help. She had to admit needing help before the facility could take her. She was only 16 and if she said no, I didn't have a clue where I'd turn next. We both went in to the see the doctor where he questioned about her drug use. Theresa was asked what her drug of choice was and she said "acid". My heart broke and tears welled up in my eyes. Never in my most wild dreams could I ever imagine this happening in my family. The doctor then asked the million-dollar question as casually as possible. "Do you think you need some help with this problem?" And she said, "I guess so." That was enough. She unknowingly signed herself in to the hospital. I stayed with her while she checked in through the clinic. Her face seemed ashen in color as I took the suitcase from the trunk of the car. She sadly and surprisingly said, "You knew you were going to leave me here." I had tears in my eyes. I nodded yes.

They would have to search the bag and anything else she brought in with her. They assigned her a number so that she could remain anonymous. She would receive any communication from us through this number in order to keep her confidentiality. The PDAP counselor and I drove home and I went into an empty house until Michael came home from school. When he heard about Theresa he just stayed in his room and kept quiet.

I cried that night and many nights afterward. Eric and I kept going to PDAP with Michael. I'd share about what was going on with Theresa at treatment and with Michael and Eric at home. Sometimes it was very hard because Eric would be sitting next to me and I wanted to share about our differences but I didn't think I could. The hardest part at this time was still having really wonderful, good people in my life but still feeling all alone and just plain hurt and angry at what life had dealt me.

Family week was very difficult also. This is a time when the family gets to visit and learn at the treatment center for one week. I could hardly believe I was in the situation I was in. At times I felt as though I was living someone else's life and at other times I thought I would wake up to my old life with all this being a dream. I still thought of Theresa as my innocent little girl. Being only 16 and so beautiful, with so much potential and in just a few short months she had changed to a withdrawn, irritated and moody person, one most people would keep their distance from.

Chris came home from college while Theresa was in rehab. School was over and it was summer. William and Ann chose to keep living in Maryland. Ann had gotten a summertime job and could live in a small group home on her college campus. William had his own apartment that he was sharing with some other college friends. He still had his job at Safeway and he also had a girlfriend. Chris was able to get a job right away here in San Antonio. He had a job interview on Monday afternoon the first day we were at family week, so he drove up separately and came late to the meeting. Michael was fourteen at the time and was able to be at family week with us. The first night was a class on the disease and how it affected the brain cells of the chemically dependent person. One important thing Eric remembers that the doctor said was that he had good news and bad news – "The bad news is about 60% of the patients who were genetically wired got the disease of addiction and about 40% of genetically predisposed people didn't get the disease. The good news is there is some choice involved in overcoming and recovering from the disease."

Most of this class was a little too much detail even for me, although I had enough science background because I was an RN. Maybe it was the feeling of being overwhelmed that blocked my ability to comprehend so much information. Regardless of why, the next several days were very intense classes about communication, emotions, defenses, dysfunctions, and family roles. Nothing can really prepare you for the intensity of this week.

The day our topic was "Family Roles" was sort of a review for me but it was so helpful to have everyone in the family hearing the same thing. I had already heard about these roles at some of the meetings I had attended in PDAP. Family members going through very stressful times will take on different roles. The stress is usually focused on the victim. In alcoholic/addicted families the alcoholic/addict is the victim. The person who is usually the closest emotionally to victim becomes the caretaker or enabler. Because these two are not emotionally (and sometimes physically) available, the hero steps in to help. He works real hard to save face in the family as well as the community. The scapegoat sees all this and diverts attention by acting out and getting in trouble. The mascot tries to lighten things up by making jokes and bring humor to the family. The lost child just leaves emotionally and physically. They go to their room or another place to be alone and get involved in something else, such as computers, books or pets, to escape. You can learn more about these roles from reading most of Sharon Wegscheider-Cruse books.

We were staying in a very comfortable hotel in a small town. Along with our room we were able to attend a fitness center across the street. Chris and Michael loved this and went there every evening they could. Sometimes they went there when Eric and I attended a meeting that really didn't involve them.

One evening we were to fill out papers that told each other how we felt. We were given an assignment to spend some time alone and answer each question the best we could. Our family started talking about what our boundaries were. Then we had to think about what the consequences were also. This gave everyone the opportunity to see how important it was that we all agreed and followed through on all our consequences – NO MATTER WHAT THE RESULTS. We worked on this throughout the week and before Theresa came home.

It all seemed like a surreal, dreamlike event for me. I was so overwhelmed with how fast this disease had taken over my daughters' and my life.

At night we all went down to the outdoor pool at the hotel. I usually would try to enjoy a quiet, refreshing swim but sometimes the emotional pain was overwhelming I would just sit and stare. One night I met a lady who was also attending family week. Her husband was in rehab and she shared her story with me. She had left her small children with their grandparents and I could not help but feel so sad. I spent a lot of time just talking with her. It seemed wherever I went I *needed* to share stories with others. There was so much value in this for me. Anyway, as a family we worked on our communication papers that night. It was a grueling assignment because of all the emotions and intensity of the week.

Before the week started I told Chris we would celebrate his birthday when we were back home. So his 19th birthday had come and it was nearly ten at night when I remembered and said "Oh, Happy Birthday Chris"!

He said "Thanks mom."

"Do you want to go next door to the Dairy Queen?"

"No", he joked. "It's too late that you remembered my birthday!"

It became our family joke about how we didn't remember his birthday and it was another indication he was "the lost child" of the family.

We did the communication exercises the next day. Each family took turns sharing their homework assignment with each other while the other families listened. They always start a sharing session by doing a feeling check with each person. I remember I said I felt "defensive". I was so afraid of getting hurt again.

When it was our family's turn to share I noticed how difficult it was on Theresa. One of the comments Theresa had made during the assignment was that she had never seen Eric and I fight until a few months earlier when it was over her drug use. To this day I think this had a profound impact on her, as well as us.

There were four families in the room that I remember. One family had two different sets of parents, the other had very religious parents, the other had a violent child and the parents reacted with physical violence and then there was our family. *At the time I thought that if I ever wrote a book it would be titled "We Don't Fit the Profile". Now I realize that all people fit the profile – no one is immune not matter how much love, prayers, money, status, power or virtues you have. This disease knows no boundaries.* I felt the burden of the day weighing heavy on my shoulders. I wasn't sure I could tolerate much more emotionally.

After dinner that evening we were getting together again for an Al-anon meeting on campus. Eric and I had an extra half hour before the meeting so we decided to walk up the hill behind the meeting room, called Serenity Hill, to see the sunset. As we walked up the dirt path holding hands, we noticed rocks along the way with some pretty harsh phrases written on them. There were things like "sexual abuse", "in memory of", "fighting" and "rages". It wasn't long before Eric and I figured out people were leaving their burdens written on stones as a symbol of starting over with a new life. As I read the rocks I could feel the pain well up inside me. I let go of Eric's hand. Was my daughter also feeling these painful burdens? Was she unable to tell me, or anyone, in the family? The joy of holding hands and going to admire the sunset was soon replaced by standing in silence in front of each and every rock -

separately - as if I was mourning each person's loss and pain. By the time I reached the top of the hill, the view didn't matter anymore. I wanted to run and hide; never to be in this place again. Eric and I looked at each other and nodded as if to say this is enough and we walked down hill in silence.

Two little old ladies who spoke to us about their experience, strength and hope held the Al-anon meeting. They told about their marriages to alcoholics who they had no control over and that they had to make the decision to take care of themselves. How hard their lives seemed also, but they spoke of joy and helping others know that working their own program was a way out of the pain. That's good because my pain was increasing by the hour as we walked through family week. On the way back to the hotel I cried uncontrollably in the car. I know Eric must have felt bad. He would reach over and hold my hand. There was nothing more neither he nor I could do.

The next day Eric, Chris, Michael, and I met with Theresa and her rehab counselor. Theresa made some amends to us and we all got to talk about things. It was so sad to hear Chris talk about how he would hear kids talking about her drug use in their high school. (Chris was a senior and Theresa was a freshman.) He would stand up for her and defend her and say there's no way she would ever use drugs. Theresa was not like that at all. He said how embarrassed he was in front of his friends when he learned that all the things they were saying were true.

Later that day, Theresa got an afternoon pass to be with the family. In 1996 there wasn't very much out in the small town, so we spent some time by the river and went to lunch at McDonalds inside the local Wal-Mart. It was Eric, myself, Chris, Theresa and Michael sitting at the lunch table. Theresa looked so cute, so young and innocent. How easy it would be to not believe all this talk of drug addiction. As we were all making conversation because at times like these it is very difficult to find common topics, Theresa matter-of-factly stated that she had been tested for HIV because she needed to be. I looked at her and saw her like she was 7 years old with pigtails swinging her feet and smiling. I saw a similar scene like that in the movie "Father of the Bride" when the dad was looking at his daughter as she told her family of her wedding plans. My heart broke and I just smiled back and asked her to let us know how it turns out.

Just a few months ago, at an education class that Theresa and I taught about the disease of addiction for the members in Family Group in PDAP, Theresa shared about one night I was driving her to a friend's house where she was meeting a boy who she was planning to have sex with. I did not know this until her talk this night! However, back in 1995, I knew something was wrong and I was feeling very frightened that night as I drove her to friends house and I talked to her about letting people use her and I told her how much I cared about her. She said because of what I said to her that night, she didn't have sex with the boy who eventually died from AIDS. This is one of those times where I think I listened to God and let go of the results and realize what ever will happen will happen.

IX. Coming Home (Boundaries)

June 1996

Theresa stayed an extra two weeks at rehab because they thought she'd benefit from that. After she was discharged, they allowed her to come home with us rather then sending her to a half-way house I think because our entire family was in recovery. *Many people who have just completed their inpatient treatment are referred to half-way houses so they can ease their way back into the "real world". The half-way houses are excellent places for a recovering person to keep very active in their recovery and at the same time start to make life skill adjustments such as getting a job or finishing school. If a recovering person is sent home to an unsupportive environment it may be too difficult to maintain sobriety.*

Just like in the half-way houses we were all working a program and were committed to working the steps and our meetings. Theresa had a Recovery Plan and each family member had a Recovery Plan. It was very important that all of us follow our own plans. She needed to go to 90 meetings in 90 days. You could count church, counseling appointments, therapy, meeting with your sponsor, PDAP functions, or meetings as something to fulfill the 90/90 requirement. Although I didn't have a 90/90 commitment for myself in writing I was practicing one daily.

She was discharged on a Tuesday, a meeting night. We went to dinner first. After dinner we attended our regular PDAP meeting. At the meeting that night I shared as usual but I really felt. I really felt... painful feelings. A deep, heavy, we're in it for the long haul, it's not going away, and my life is – has somehow changed forever...feeling. At "coffee", the place we socialize after the meeting, Theresa stayed close by my side. She sat with the parents and she looked so ashen white again and she was so quiet. I wanted to hug her and say it will be all right. But I continued to just do my normal thing talking mostly with moms. My need to replace my obsession of my child became one of working through my own pain. Where to let go and let God and when to hear God and act had become a daily struggle. At the time just letting Theresa be and letting her adjust seemed to be the best action to take. When we got home at 10:30 that night we had a cake to celebrate Theresa's homecoming. We were happy to have her home.

Joanne D.

We had written a list of boundaries while we were at family week. Chris, Michael, Eric and I all agreed about calling the police if Theresa didn't follow certain rules. The rules were listed on the refrigerator.

Here is what we said:

Rules and Consequences

1. *No Drugs or alcohol in the house or carried on you — we will call the police or send you to another rehab to get more help.*
2. *If we find drugs or paraphernalia — we will call the police.*
3. *If you go out without permission — we will call missing persons and list you as a runaway.*
4. *If you go out with kids we don't approve of — we will call the police or missing persons. (This one is good only if you actually don't know where your child is, so don't try to find out. You can't say they're missing if you know where they are.)*
5. *You must attend 2 PDAP meetings/week, 1 counseling session/week, and 1 activity/week as part of the 90/90 or we will send you to another rehab.*
6. *You must follow the San Antonio curfew or we will report you.*
7. *No parental advisory CD's — we will destroy and throw them away.*
8. *If you don't go to school — we will report you to school authorities.*

It is good to write your list and talk it over with someone who knows about addiction. Some other rules and consequences have to do with cursing and disrespect. If this happens some parents say they will not respond or be helpful to their children until the respect is there.

It is also good to make copies of your rules because these papers often disappear!

Did you notice there was nothing about grades or cleaning your room? For my family this wasn't a boundary. However it was very difficult for me to tolerate. The grades I had to work on letting go and letting the school give the consequence, but the messiness I got creative. Anything that Theresa, or Michael for that matter, left lying around the house I would pick up and throw in the garage. My house was clean and they were a little put out that they had to go hunting for their things out in the garage.

If your loved one is over 18, not in school and living at home, the issue of work generally comes up. A good rule and consequence is to have you child pay a small fee (like $25.00/week) on a specific date (like starting the first of the month) for room and board. This leaves a lot of the thinking and footwork up to your child and keeps you out of the picture. Your child has some dignity in finding his/her own job, no matter how small because their only goal right now is to pay that small fee. The rest will come later as they gain strength in sobriety. You also have to be willing to follow through with the consequence and "evict" them if they don't pay.

X. Summer 1996

One evening while Eric, Theresa and Michael were out, I asked Chris if he wanted to go to the movies. This was part of my doing something for fun at least once a week (whether I needed it or not) and I can't remember the last time I went to the movies with Chris. He said he'd go with me. We arrived early for the show and we were alone in the theater. I started to share with him about how I was doing so much better since I started going to PDAP and that I thought I had been depressed for such a long time. I told him I had so much more hope now. The PDAP counselor had told me that I might be somewhat obsessive/compulsive. He listened and then said to me that he understood exactly what I was telling him. Just a few days earlier, Chris had read somewhere about the symptoms of

Obsessive-Compulsive Disorder. By saying these words Chris took a risk and talked about something that had been bothering him for a long time. He told me about when he was in sixth grade and he had come to me to tell me about his strange feelings that he couldn't really describe other than something was wrong with him. I had taken him to the family doctor and the doctor suggested that I take Chris off a decongestant he was taking. Chris never said anything about this again until one day when he was in eleventh grade and we were in the car going to Drivers Ed. A truck had accidentally dropped bolts all over the highway. There was no way of avoiding the bolts and cars slowed down to drive through this sea of metal debris.

At this time Chris said "Mom, do you remember in sixth grade when I told you something was wrong with me and you took me to the doctor."

"Yes, Chris, I do."

"Well, those strange feelings never really went away. I don't know what they are. But, I still get them."

I felt a little nervous and I tried to sound neutral when I said this, however, I know I sounded negative. "Well, do you think you need a psychiatrist or something?"

He was quiet and then said, "No, I don't think so."

(That was the right answer as far as I was concerned.)

I told Chris I remembered all that. "Well, Mom, it's getting worse. I still don't know what's wrong. But I don't think I can go back to school in the fall. I'm afraid I'll 'crash'". I felt so much compassion and understanding this time because of all I had gone through. I had some fear but I certainly wanted to get Chris help. The thought of a psychiatrist for my child didn't scare me at all. The next day, I got with a counselor at PDAP and got the names of some therapists to get Chris help. He got started in therapy right away and was going every day and sometimes twice a day. He was diagnosed with Obsessive Compulsive Disorder (OCD).

The week after Theresa got out of rehab there were classes being given each day at PDAP for the kids. Since Theresa was "willing" at this time it wasn't difficult to get her to go to meetings. These classes also fulfilled her requirements to attend 90 meetings in 90 days. As time progressed there were days she didn't want to get up or go to a PDAP outing.

One day the group was going to the zoo and Theresa said she really didn't want to go. My thought for the day was to do my 1% and let God do the other 99%. So I did my part and brought her to the PDAP building and left her there. She had argued with me on the way over and I told her to just go in and ask the PDAP counselors if it's ok to leave because your part was to do something for recovery every day. She could call me when I needed to come get her. (This was before using cell phones was common.) She went inside and I left. As I drove home I prayed for the strength do to the right thing and I prayed the Serenity Prayer. The Beetles song "Let It Be" came on the radio and I knew God was taking care of everything. I expected a message from Theresa on the answering machine asking me to pick her up and there was none. As time passed I imagined that she had gone to the zoo very reluctantly and was having a miserable time. However, I kept the prayers to keep me focused on God's will *for me* and He would take care of Theresa also. Late in the day she called and asked to be picked up. I went to get her and did not mention how worried I had been all day. She, however, talked about the nice day she had at the zoo. It was a good lesson for me to realize how my worry makes me sick and does not help the situation. I started to let go of my mantra – Hang on and Help God!

I went to Maryland to visit William and Ann and also to go visit my family in Connecticut. While I was away my husband, Eric had his first encounter with calling the police. Eric and I talked daily as I visited with my family. One day he called to say that he had to call the police on Theresa. Theresa had called Eric at work and defiantly said she was going over her girlfriends' house that she used to do drugs with. Eric told her no because her friend was still using drugs. One of the boundaries we had was if you go out with someone who uses drugs we will call the police. The officer was very nice to Eric and explained that there was basically nothing he could do because Eric knew where she was but he would talk to her if Eric wanted him to. Eric called Theresa and said he had called the police and the police would go out there to talk to her. He said she seemed scared and she would come home. *The main point of this story is that if you give consequences make sure you follow through, so that your word will mean something.*

It was difficult for me to let go of what was going on at home while I was in Connecticut. I really needed a break from the constant stress of the situation at home. No matter how much I enjoyed the company of William, Ann and my family, the pain of the reality of addiction was sometimes unbearable. When I left William and Ann, I felt a deep sense of loss. It was a loss of life as it used to be and of dreams of what might have been. On the plane flight home I felt my mind growing dark as I reached out to God. Looking back I think I was becoming clinically depressed. I had a sense that I was looking at the world from a place further back in my brain. I had to keep imagining that God was right next to me, with me, in me and I repeated over and over that it would be all right. I felt intense loneliness as I tried to not take on Theresa's illness and to convince myself that I was a good mom.

I was getting ready to do my inventory. This is Step 5 in PDAP. I had spent many hours reading and writing before the trip and while away I spent a lot of time in prayer. I was working my program like my life depended on it. I guess because my life depended on it.

School would be starting soon and I knew that would a big trigger for Theresa. I prayed for the strength to get through it all. I started to realize how much fear was taking over and that I really needed to replace all that fear with faith. I also realized that although I had faith in God I did not have faith in the outcome of how things would turn out for Theresa in her disease.

I realized that my belief in everything turning out good, if I believed in God, was false. Bad things do happen to good and faithful people. Job, from the bible, became my hero. I also clung to the idea that Adam and Eve were the first parents and one of their children killed the other. There wasn't MTV or concerts with foul language, sexual content and drug abuse. There is very definitely evil in the world and it attacks every one of us at some time. However, what I have come to realize is that all things work for good through God, but I have to be open and willing.

I was anxious to get moving on the PDAP fifth step. I had been raised Catholic and I realized the benefit of confession. Although I still received this sacrament I hadn't learned to really communicate my true beliefs about my wrong doing. I was taught very simply about telling my sins in a grocery list type of way. The new way of sitting face to face and telling a priest really didn't change things for me except I felt more shame. I said the same sins and I really never looked past the action. This fifth step in PDAP had me looking at my action, what it affected and what pattern was seen throughout all these self-defeating behaviors.

It was the third day after started school in August 1996. I had been planning this day for several weeks. My sponsor was coming over in the morning to hear my inventory. Just a few minutes before my sponsor was due to be at my house, the school called. They were just confirming Theresa's absence from school the day before and today.

"No", I said. "She should be there, in school."

I knew Theresa had talked about seeing her friend, Dana, in school so I called her house. I asked her mom if she knew if her daughter was in school both days. Her mom called the school and called right back to say her daughter had been absent also.

It took all the courage I had at the time to tell Dana's mom about Theresa being in a drug rehab and being a drug addict. I explained that we were in a program right now and that Theresa was on very shaky ground. She had stayed sober all summer and was trying her best to keep it that way now. Theresa also used drugs with Dana just before she went to rehab.

After this conversation, my sponsor called to say she was in the neighborhood and would be there any minute. I was already emotionally exhausted from this phone call and really had lost my desire to share my inventory with anyone. I have no idea why I went ahead with it but I did.

This is the PDAP sixth step. There wasn't much fear or guilt in anything I had done, so I moved forward in getting through this step. I had everything in writing. I did the best I could as far as remembering past wrongs. It seemed my biggest resentments were at my husband, for moving, and the time he devoted to his career. There was resentment about Theresa, and Michael's, using drugs. I looked at a lot of my caretaking and control issues and also some self-esteem issues.

After finishing my inventory I was to spend an hour alone with God and review what I said and if I had been thorough. I cried. I cried for hours and it was uncontrollable.

By the time Eric came home from work he said I'd better call my sponsor because I looked awful. My sponsor told me I was okay and I was grounded. I found this very confusing. On the one hand, I knew God was with me and I was truly grounded in God but on the other hand, I was full of fear and pain and more emotions than words could express. At this same time I was trying to keep it together and talk to Theresa. When Theresa came home from school we talked about what was going on with her in school. She was more open to talking, now that she had been sober for a few months. I called the school the next day and the school counselor changed a class that was causing Theresa hardship. This seemed to help temporarily.

I could not stop the Pandora's Box of emotions that followed. Day after day I spent hours crying. I started to lose sleep at night and I started to sleep more in the daytime. I am so grateful that I took 2 morning classes in college for that year otherwise I don't think I would have gotten out of bed. Also the homework gave me something else to focus on. I also taught religion once a week to fifth graders at my church.

I simply just kept walking through the pain. And the pain got worse. A few months later, as I stepped out of the shower, I froze for a second, as an image of a man over my bed came into my mind. It reminded me of movies about people having flashbacks. Not that I would have a flashback because there would be nothing to have a flashback about. My life was pretty much perfect until this drug addiction problem, wasn't it?

Theresa was doing much better after the Dana incident. Dana's mom put her in treatment and Theresa's guidance counselor changed some of her classes so she was not with the kids who tempted her the most. Michael was doing great also. As a family we all went to meetings and functions and kept working our steps.

In the fall, Eric and I went to a marriage workshop we had heard about from people in recovery. It was way down in South Padre Island, about a four or five hour drive from San Antonio. Our kids were doing well. Theresa had been sober since the first week of school and Michael had been adding beads to his fist. (Each bead stands for another month sober.) He was about 6 months sober.

Our thought was to go for the weekend but not tell the kids we'd be gone that long. We would be able to come home at any time. We planned a PDAP party for the kids at our house for Friday night, that way there would be PDAP counselors with them. One of the single PDAP counselors would spend the night at our house. Saturday, as usual for our kids, they would sleep and so our next problem would be Saturday night. A friend from the group invited the kids over to spend Saturday night. Then we waited until Saturday night to tell them we'd be home the next morning. It was very manipulative and controlling on our part but if for any reason things did not go well we would have left the workshop.

The workshop did us a world of good. I don't remember the topic or much else except the therapist drew a triangle. Each spouse was at the bottom of the triangle and God was at the top. If we both worked toward reaching God then we would be okay.

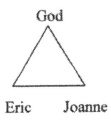

Our plan seemed to have worked so well that we stayed at South Padre Island another night so we could have a day just for fun. The kids stayed at their PDAP friends' house one more night. The emotional pain was beginning to occur even when I was in public now. It used to be just a private thing. I didn't tell Eric about how strong the feelings were because I kept thinking and hoping they would go away. I thought I was having the pain all the parents were experiencing and maybe I was just being a wimp. With the workshop being over we spent a day on the pier fishing. It was relaxing for me because I let the warm sun remind me of God's love and that we were where we needed to be. I would keep striving for God's will!

XI. Our First Family Retreat

November 1996

The next month, November, Eric, Theresa, Michael and I were on a family retreat. Although things kept improving with the family, things inside me seemed to be getting worse. Michael had turned 15 on this weekend. There was a PDAP tradition for the group to hold the birthday teenager down and dump food and gooey things on a person. Michael had saved a long time to get some really good shoes. The new shoes pretty much got ruined during this process. They had given me chocolate syrup to be part of the "fun" and it was very difficult but I poured it on him. I regret this today and I guess I owe an amends. It was also the last time the group practiced this tradition!

The really moving part of this weekend was when we all washed each others feet like at the Last Supper and a PDAP counselor washed Theresa's feet and Theresa got to wash Eric's feet and Eric washed Michael's feet. I was left out but that was okay with me to see my family start to heal. Theresa left the meeting and she was gone for a while so I went to check on her. I found her crying in the bathroom but she wouldn't talk to me. I started crying also. I thought of Chris, who got help in therapy and me who was feeling all of MY feelings and not trying to feel for my children, and I said, "Theresa do you know what you've done for our family?" "We're all getting help now!"

After a few minutes of crying we both went back in to the meeting room. There Theresa, Michael, Eric and I all hugged each and cried out loud as we sat on the floor. I didn't know what would ever become of us but I knew we loved each other and no one or no thing could take that away – not even the disease of addiction.

Well that being said and being very profound for all of us. The other issue for me was still rather overbearing. I felt emotional pain that would not stop and I wanted to somehow stop it. This retreat was part camp-out and part cabins. Eric had a tent and he wanted me to stay with him. I had been so dependant on Eric for every thing since he had been my only friend for 23 years and now I was pulling away. I saw how much this pained him and I did not know how to have both girlfriends and him. I needed the other women in the group so much. It felt like my life depended on it. The pain and strain in our marriage was getting worse. I stayed in a cabin and he slept out in the tent. What was wrong with me?

XII. Post Traumatic Stress Disorder

(PTSD)

My first flashback happened while I was stepping out of the shower. I froze as I opened the shower door and an image of a bright light in the ceiling and the face of a man above me. My heart skipped a beat and I shook the thoughts loose as fear and pain welled up inside me. I got dressed in pj's and hid in my bed. I thought if anyone knew what was going on in my mind I would surely end up in a mental hospital

The pain, the flashbacks and then the continuing nightmares never seemed to let up. So many nights before the inventory I had restless nights worrying about Theresa – wondering what she was doing up in the middle of the night with her light on or waiting up for her if she had snuck out. I continually worried about my daughter, fearing for her life because of drug addiction. Now, my nightmares changed from horrible images of my child and the rest of my family in despair, to images of me being trapped, attacked and physically hurt. I would wake up in tears sometimes yelling, sometimes trying to yell through frozen lips which sounded like terrifying mumbling. Many times I'd be afraid to go to sleep because it was so painful. I felt like I was haunted by memories awake or asleep and the pain kept getting worse.

I wasn't sure if I should tell Eric. I was afraid at first, that he would get real upset and be convinced that I really did need to be in a mental hospital and then I would think maybe I should admit myself to a mental hospital. I really think I was just looking for a way to stop the pain, and a mental hospital would probably have drugs along with therapy that would help.

This started happening around December 1996. I didn't understand this fear and panic and now images passing before my eyes, which later I would learn were flashbacks. Right now I was unable to discern the reality of a memory and something that was free floating through my mind.

William and Ann would be coming home from college for Christmas to visit and I wanted to have things like they used to be. I was so excited see them. With all the things going on inside me I was still keeping the secret of what my pain might be about except to the counselor at PDAP. I wanted so much to lead a normal life and I started to believe I was having "wrong thoughts" and somehow I could gain control over my thoughts and feelings just by keeping my focus on working the steps, talking, sharing, praying, meditating and journaling. I would get reprieves from the pain and whenever the emotional pain returned I would start to think "the painful feelings" were my enemy. The thoughts and feelings rarely ever went together and I did my best to avoid either of them.

I kept appointments with the drug abuse counselor and she kept recommending I see a therapist. My fear of admitting I had a mental problem or disorder was so great that I was in constant conflict. I remember when I was a young girl, about 13. My maternal grandfather had died a year earlier and my paternal grandmother had just past away. I was driving in the car with my father and I asked him where my grandfather, his father, was buried. I assumed since I had never seen or heard about him that he must be dead. He was silent for a bit and then said he wasn't dead. This was a surprise. So I asked where he was. "He's in a hospital." (It was a mental hospital, but they could not even say the word and even today I have a hard time disclosing it.)

Well, that was more of a surprise.

"Why don't we go visit him?" I asked.

"Because we can't, we don't tell anyone about him."

Wow! That was a lot to process. I had a grandfather that I didn't know about somewhere in a hospital. When we arrived home I asked my mother if she knew about grandpa. She acknowledged she did by saying to my father "you told her?" She was obviously upset and said I should never tell anyone because no one needs to know that. When I asked if we could visit him or why nobody ever did visit I was told that we just didn't.

Years later I learned it probably didn't matter to my grandfather if anyone was there because he probably didn't know anyone anyway. But at the time it was clear to me that mental illness was a secret and shameful.

Christmas that year with the kids was wonderful. Theresa had been sober since the end of October and Michael had been staying sober since he entered the program, about 9 months earlier. We looked really good on the outside, even though I know I was in a lot of pain and that others in the family were also. Now I can see we were being changed from the inside out.

Chris was in therapy since August and from my conversations with him he was improving in his ability to cope. I was gaining confidence in the fact that mental disorders are a sickness like anything else. I had very little understanding about what Chris was going through and from what I understood about Obsessive/ Compulsive Disorder (OCD) the person internalizes all the feelings he/she can't cope with and focuses the pain on something external. This helps transfer what they don't want to feel. At times I would feel huge waves of guilt over the fact that that I couldn't be there for Chris emotionally when he was a child because there was so much going on in our house. I would feel extreme sadness for the little boy who didn't want to cause problems.

Almost daily, I kept having flashbacks, body memories and emotional pain. I was losing concentration on everything, sleeping is what I tried to do in the daytime and found impossible to do at night. I had so many nightmares and everyday seemed harder than the day before. Sometimes Eric and I would drive out to the country to see Eric's sponsor and his wife. We'd have to drive through corn fields and I think this became a trigger for me. When I was little girl I spent a week at my aunts farm house. The room I stayed in was downstairs and faced the backyard – the corn field. There was an image of a man standing over me. The man I was never supposed to talk to, I was supposed to stay away from him. Looking back I think he was an alcoholic but nobody said so. He began to be in my dreams and I felt haunted.

Along with these thoughts and feelings I saw my dad when he was very angry. Also I had sad and lonely feelings of growing up as a caretaker. I would help take care of everyone else. When I was eight years old my aunt was very sick and she found out she was pregnant with her fifth child. My mom helped her a lot. After the baby was born my aunt was diagnosed with Multiple Sclerosis. My baby cousin came to live with our family and my mother was pregnant. One day, my grandfather, who also lived with us, fell over the banister while he was carrying my baby cousin down the stairs. My cousin hit her head on the foot of the radiator and the "soft spot" on her head began to swell almost as big as her head. My parents rushed her off to the hospital.

The house was empty except for grandpa and me. Grandpa sat on the couch downstairs praying out loud in German. I was sitting on top of the stairs. I could see his feet through the stair rails and when I bent way down I could see all of him. He was praying the "Our Father". I recognized some words and then I began to whisper the prayer along with him.   He was so sad. He would have moments of crying and go back praying. It was then I knew there was a God and that nothing would ever take that away from me. He was there in that house with grandpa and me, as well as out there with my parents, and baby cousin, who might or might not live.

Looking back we think grandpa probably had a minor stroke but didn't realize it. Several weeks later he had a serious car accident (we think a major stroke occurred) and he was listed in critical condition in another hospital. My aunt was dying in yet another hospital. My parents were extremely busy and I tried to help them as much as I could. My aunt died soon after, my cousin came home from the hospital after months of care and my grandfather did also. My grandfather needed constant care for the next four years after his accident. My baby brother was born, and a year later a baby sister and two years later another baby brother. My mom still talks about how much help I was when I was young. Caretaking was survival skill I learned very well.

Joanne D.

Our one year lease was up in December 1996 and at that time we started to look for a cheaper house. We had made many moves, many of which I handled alone. So I looked in the paper and made a few phone calls. I wasn't having any luck finding a cheaper house to rent and when I told Eric it was almost impossible to find a place, he made a phone call, got an answer and had a realtor looking for us. I was devastated that I couldn't even do something that was so easy for me all my life.

As time passed I began to have anxiety attacks but I didn't know what they were. I became afraid to go to the store and I had a hard time remembering what I was there for. What was wrong with me? I had raised five kids! Shopping, especially for food, was second nature to me. I did what I had to do but it was getting more and more difficult. I couldn't put off going to see a therapist anymore.

Soon it was Valentines Day and Eric and I were alone. Theresa, Michael and Chris were out for the evening. Eric and I lit a fire and things were very peaceful. No stress or worries or things to do, just relaxing. The emotional pain crept up and started to overtake me now. I tried to share with Eric but I had so much fear, so much of a of a "no talk" rule. Eric listened and was very understanding. I had such a fear he would put me in a mental hospital and such a fear that's where I belonged and I should put myself there. That's all I could take. The very next morning I called for an appointment with a therapist.

68

XIII. Therapy

February 1997

I vaguely remember my first appointment with my therapist. I cried as I tried to explain some of what was going on. My therapist calmly said, "Joanne, I think you're depressed." "I want you to see a doctor about getting on some medication." We talked more and I returned a week later. My therapist asked if I had seen a doctor and I explained to her that I didn't think I was depressed because I was much worse the year before as far as sadness goes. "I'm doing so much better." She very firmly said "You need to see a doctor." My big concern was having to tell my whole story over to someone else. I didn't think I could tell another human being that I might have something mentally wrong with me.

The old painful memories of not talking about mental illness and the stigma attached to it were taking over. Now my therapist was not asking, she was telling me to go to another individual for help.

It took every ounce of courage for me to call Behavioral Medicine on the military base for an appointment. The military hospital did not feel like a safe place to go for help. I had a fear that my appointment might reflect on Eric at work. Many old tapes played in my head from not telling people our problems to how this might affect Eric's career. My thoughts kept pulling me down more. By the time I reached the doctor's office it was hard to stop the tears. The doctor wrote me a prescription for Prozac. "Oh no, didn't someone try to kill themselves while they were on Prozac?" Then I thought I really don't need this, I'm okay. Eric kept encouraging me to at least try the medication. It couldn't hurt and it might help. I put off filling the prescription for a few days until I realized that this was an opportunity to change and I didn't want to keep doing the same thing. Wasn't the definition for insanity this – doing the same thing over and over again expecting different results?

When I took the medication, the results were immediate. I felt some relief after the first dose. Not much, but some, and with each passing day on medication I felt just a little better. I didn't realize that the emotional pain I felt was causing a stinging in my hands and feet as well as the rest of my body. The anxiety lessened daily.

When I saw a friend at a meeting she was surprised to see such a difference in my appearance. I know the medication should have taken between 4-6 weeks to take affect but I was truly feeling somewhat lighter.

For my third visit to my therapist I got to say I was taking my medication and it was already having a small affect on my well-being. I could feel myself moving from the back of my head slowly toward the front. It took many months but the darkness surrounding my thoughts cleared. I still had my feelings and I cried daily but my head was not full of darkness and confusion. Slowly with the mix of medication and therapy I could feel my feelings and put a name on them and thoughts that went with them.

So began my journey through repressed childhood emotional, physical and sexual abuse issues. Various flashbacks, painful feelings and thoughts were an every day occurrence. One afternoon Eric and I were out having lunch with some of our kids. It was a fun time but the emotional "painful feelings" kept distracting me and finally I had to go call my therapist. When I called from a pay phone outside the restaurant, my therapist asked me where I was. Not being that familiar with San Antonio yet, I answered I was somewhere in San Antonio. She very calmly said "that's good". I realized how disoriented that sounded and I laughed. In the program we try to live in the present moment but when you go through traumatic events those moments get so confusing that it feels very "crazy". Sometimes I would ask my therapist to admit me to a mental hospital and sometimes I feared it.

My children were doing alright but I was struggling to exist. I began to turn on Eric at times and I wanted to be with women only. I began to fear most men and since Eric was one of them I wanted to avoid him. Sometimes just being with him triggered flashbacks.

My therapist told me about a book called "The Courage to Heal" and suggested I read it. Eric and I were at the bookstore and I saw the book. It was even a traumatic event to pick the book up. The fear inside was so strong. If I read this book would I admit to this really having happened to me or would I get more ideas and feel more painful feelings? After struggling inside for awhile I asked Eric if he would pick it up and buy it for me. Thankfully he was willing to support me and he purchased the book. It sat on the shelf for a long time before I ventured to read it. My therapist also said there was a book for my husband to read called "Ghosts in the Bedroom" which we purchased and it really helped Eric which in turn helped me. Ever since this time Eric would always say "this is a safe bed" and he meant it.

XIV. Spring 1997

In March of 1997 we packed up and moved into a cheaper home. We were still paying for the three kids in college and our rehab bill left us absolutely no savings and in debt. There was no way I could even think about working. Many afternoons I would be rolled up in a ball lying on the couch hoping to find some relief in sleep or daydreams.

I struggled daily. My therapist let me borrow a video by Marilyn Van Debur Attler on sexual abuse. I watched that video over and over again for two weeks. Eric joined me on some occasions. It was difficult for me to believe a nice girl like a Miss America participant could have been abused by her father and she was talking about it openly, openly to a group of professionals and allowing it to be taped. It gave me some validation that maybe things can be repressed in your mind and they don't come out until later in your adult life. It was like secrets that I didn't even know were secret about me. I guess this was the beginning of acceptance.

One afternoon the emotional pain was so deep I had called my therapist. She called me back later in the afternoon. As I sat on the floor, I tried to talk but the words wouldn't come out. I whispered "I can't talk". She asked me if I wanted to get a drink of water. As I tried to get up I realized I was paralyzed on my bedroom floor and I said in a soft voice "I can't move". I cannot describe in words what it is like to know what's happening around you but being unable to participate in your own life. The emotional turmoil was so great I just tried to bear the pain and was so grateful for a therapist who would listen.

At this time Theresa was sober 5 months and Michael received his 1 year fist at PDAP. *A fist is a mariners knot, or a monkeys' fist, tied on the end of a leather thong that the drug users get when they are sober for 1 month and then again when they are sober for 1 year, only the thong is braided for the 1 year. The knot on the end of a heavy rope is what the mariners use to throw from ship to shore as the boat is being docked on dry land. The PDAP fist represents the drug user's first contact with sobriety being pulled in, out of the sea of drugs and alcohol.* Theresa had received her fist 1 month after rehab but then the relapse when school started made her ineligible to wear it until sometime in December when she had been sober for 1 month again. So for the time being both Theresa and Michael were sober. Theresa was going out with the same boy for a few months now and they seemed very committed to one another. Her boyfriend had an older brother and a younger sister and the 5 of them became the best of friends and sober support for each other.

My role as a mother was not as stressful as it was when I started in PDAP. I was able to let go and let other people help. My role as a wife, however, was killing me. In therapy I learned I was going through PTSD and recovery from sexual abuse. I basically became so afraid of men in general and Eric specifically. He sort of represented the enemy though I knew in my heart what a good man he was. Some of the things I would do to push Eric away would be to start an argument with him, ignore him or just plain stay away from him. I must also say that I really had a strong desire to be with other women and share the pain of a child's addiction. I felt great comfort in sharing with them and just plain talking about my problems.

XV. Meeting a New Neighbor

April 1997

One day just after we had moved into our new neighborhood I was out in front planting flowers in the garden. We moved to a house in the same school district to make things easier for Theresa and Michael. I met very few people through school. My conversations were with teachers about Theresa's or Michael's problems. It didn't make sense to go to open school nights or PTA meetings when I was barely functioning and I had constant contact with the school almost on a weekly basis because of the trouble they'd get into. I missed the old days terribly.

Anyway, as I was outside our new home on this beautiful spring day gardening, a lady stopped by to say hello and welcome me to the neighborhood. She was very talkative and I felt very relaxed with her. After 10 or 15 minutes I invited her in for a glass of iced tea. She told me all about her teenagers' school activities and then asked me about my children - what were their interests. I told her my kids had gotten into drugs a few years back and now my kids were in a program trying to stay sober everyday. I wanted to tell her about PDAP and all it had done for my family. However, she looked at her watch and said "Look at the time. I have to go." I hadn't told her much of anything. She got up and said "good-bye". No "I'll give you a call" or "Let's get together again". It was just plain obvious that was too much information. She thanked me for the iced tea and I never saw her again. I felt rejected and always on guard after this when talking about drug abuse or alcoholism with people outside my PDAP Group.

XVI. Tubing on the River

Later that summer while we were tubing on the river after a pretty long rainy season, I almost lost my life. It was during this experience I realized I that I had to keep on doing the next right thing and that every day was truly a gift from God. The river was flowing faster than usual because of some rain storms so the tubing company bused us up the river where the water wasn't as rough and we were to get out of the river at their facility. I was with a friend I had made in the group. She was there with her three younger children. Her 13 year old went off on his own and her other 2 children who were 9 and 5 stayed with us. We floated and had fun until we came to a tree that had been overturned during a recent flood. The current had brought us to the back of the tree where all the dirt and roots were blocking the river. My friend started to push out to go back into the rivers current and I was planning to pass her children out to her so we could continue on our journey. As I turned to the child on my left I watched her go under the massive tree roots and dirt, and at the same time I watched my friend being swept out of sight with a shocked expression on her face. Then the 5 year old was swept under water and I was left all alone for just a second before I too was sucked under with such power. My thoughts raced as I thought of being swept into one of the children and hurting them. I thought that a current this strong was bound to be stopped by a large rock or wall and I would surely smash into that. I thought of all the letting go and letting God slogans I learned in the program. There was nothing else I could do. I thought of all therapy I had been through and the pain I was still carrying and how in the end it wouldn't matter to anyone but me. It seemed endless and I feared running out of air when I felt the surface of the water just above me. My head popped up and there was my friend. She was about 30 yards down river and she had the same shocked expression on her face.

She was facing me but looking passed me. I followed her line of vision and saw the backside of the tree we were sucked under. I was maybe 100 yards upstream. There was no sign of the children. I looked back at my friend and I noticed she was basically running in place. I turned to do my best to head up stream to recover the children and I could see why she wasn't getting anywhere. The current was too strong. I yelled at the top of my lungs for help. Surely people had to be headed this way, though most people were ahead us because we just moved slowly.

Still no sign of the kids. I was making some progress moving up stream. There was very little sunshine in this area of the river yet just above the tree roots the sun shined and a little head popped up out of the backside of the tree and then another. It had a heavenly appearance like angels were watching over the children. They were both alive and holding onto the brush. There swimming vests had kept them afloat as the current pulled them through the tree roots.

"Let go" we yelled "we'll catch you as you float down stream". I grabbed the 9 year old as she came toward me and then my friend got hold of the 5 year old. By this time several people had come back up stream to help and others had floated down toward us. The young girl and I found an area on the side of the river and I held her as she and I cried. Others gathered and my friend was also in tears. If it were up to me I'd be done with tubing but we had to continue to get back. One of the men in the group took the 5 year old and held him in his tube where he drifted off to sleep after a few minutes. My friend and I and her 9 year old held each others tubes and floated back to safety with the rest of the group.

This friend and I met a lot to do step work. She shared a lot about angels that she heard helped people. She told me a story about a baby in a hospital crib that was dying and a mom crying by her bedside. The mom was praying for God to spare her child's life. She claimed to have seen a light that looked angelic above the baby and then the baby was better. As my friend shared this story I wondered why God didn't send angels to all children who are prayed over and why sexual abuse would happen at all to any child at all. No child deserves that. All the painful feelings came rushing back. My friend asked me if I was alright.

"No", I said. "I was having a difficult time." I was starting to share some of the trauma I had experienced with others in the group. I took a chance in sharing what I was going through with my friend. I started to explain my pain and I guess she saw the look on my face and she got scared. She also said she had to go and left me in a hurry. Not everyone is ready to talk about this.

At this point it was hard to tell if I was going to meetings for having children on drugs or childhood trauma. Many times I felt as though I was going backwards as far as feeling very painful feelings. Others in the group seemed to be moving much faster and not working on themsclves half as hard.

XVII. Mexico City

It was August of 1997 and my brother was getting married in Mexico City, Mexico. The wedding was to take place the first weekend after school started in August. Theresa was a senior in the ACE (Alternative in Creative Education) program and Michael was in the 11th grade. William and Ann were working in Maryland and Chris was a sophomore at University of Texas at San Antonio. Even though Marks' wedding would be during the first week of school, we decided to take the whole family if they wanted to attend. William, my son, and Ann, would fly from Maryland on Friday night and meet us there and we would all fly back to the states together. Chris, Michael and Theresa would fly out with us right after school on Wednesday. They would miss two days of school but I had hoped for a better year since the kids were now sober; almost a year for Theresa and over that for Michael. Little did I know that Michael was starting to use drugs at this time.

This is what happened. Theresa decided the week before the Wedding that she wanted to stay in school and work at her job and not go with us. This was okay with us. She was becoming more trustworthy as far as using drugs were concerned and following through on doing what she said she would do. She hadn't proved herself in many responsibilities like caring for her room or the house in general, but concern for her job seemed to be one of the first signs of maturing. It was the morning of our trip. Eric, Chris, Michael and I were all packed. I had written the high school a note saying I would take Michael out of his last class that day.

Eric and I were having lunch. We were so excited about this trip and that our family was finally starting to change from all drug use, lies and bad behavior. The phone rang and it was the high school confirming that Michael was home sick.

"No," I said. "Michael went to school this morning and I was supposed to pick him up early from school." There was a hesitation, a silence, and I said "do whatever you have to do for skipping school." They said they would "follow procedure" – whatever that was.

The phone rang again and a friend from PDAP was calling to wish us a safe trip. I told her what had happened. We hung up and Eric and I started to discuss what to do next. If Michael came home we would all continue to Mexico but there would have to be consequences. My friend that I had just talked to called back with some information from her son. He had talked to Michael. Michael had cut school and was really afraid that we knew he cut school and he wasn't coming home.

We didn't know what to do. I wanted so much to see my brother get married and see William and Ann and the rest of my family in Mexico City. I knew I couldn't leave Theresa and Michael home alone, mostly because of all the trouble they could get into and we wouldn't even be in the country. We made a decision to go anyway and take care of ourselves, yet not neglect our parental responsibilities. We called the PDAP counselor that had stayed at our house once before. We asked if he would mind staying at our house even if our kid didn't come home and he would have to be called in as a runaway. The PDAP counselor was fine with this and things were set up either way. We left a note with PDAP counselor that gave him permission to do whatever he thought appropriate to take care of Michael including calling the police. We drove to the high school just incase Michael would be waiting outside. No, he wasn't there. We drove on to the airport.

One last phone call home – no answer. One last phone call to the PDAP counselor to let him know he's in charge of our wayward child. We got on the plane and had a layover in Houston. Remember the three friends that my kids got sober and stayed sober with? Well, they were living temporarily in Houston now and they and their mother surprised us at the airport. Only they had just talked to Michael and found out that there was a hit man out to get him. Eric and I turned to each other and I said "I think the PDAP counselor can handle this much better than we could. I'm glad I'm not home right now."

It was very scary knowing so much was going on at home. I think this was one my first experiences with taking care of myself and knowing that I provided what I could and didn't compromise my needs. I can honestly look back on the happy times in my life and say this trip was one of them. I called home once when we arrived and found out Michael was safe at home. The consequence of Michael cutting school was whatever the school gave him and the consequence of him not showing up for the trip to Mexico City was that he missed a wonderful vacation.

The rest of our vacation was really good but the pain of leaving our kids in San Antonio while we were out of the country would come back every few hours. It was such a mixed bag being with my three college kids and not having my two high school kids with me. I really practiced living in the moment and not worrying about the "what ifs" during this time.

The school year from August1997 through May 1998 had some ups and downs. Theresa was a senior at ACE and Michael was a junior in high school. There were times when I wondered if they were using drugs or not but it seemed like all the rules were being respected so I basically enforced consequences and let go and let God as best I could.

At times my emotional pain would still be unbearable even though everyone around me was doing so well. Eric took me out for my birthday in September, to see John Denver in Concert at the Majestic Theater. It was very exciting for me because we had always had to be so careful with our money. Although we were still in debt Eric wanted to make my birthday special. So we splurged. The show was wonderful and I felt like I was being treated like a princess. However, the pain inside crept in slowly again and before I realized what was happening I could barely sit still in my seat. I felt emotional pain in my heart, a lump in my throat and a gnawing, throbbing pain in my hands and feet. I was having some flashbacks along with the painful feelings now. I wanted to run, to cry, and to scream and I wanted to enjoy and be present to the show at the same time. I could certainly hide my feelings on the inside so well. I'd smile at Eric and keep hoping the pain would go away.

I continued in therapy and shared my feelings, and thoughts that went with them, with my therapist.

XVIII. New Years Eve

The last day 1997 was quite interesting. We were getting ready to go to a PDAP dance. Every New Years Eve PDAP does some fun event and this year it was a dance. Michael was accused of stealing a girl's purse so Eric searched Michael's room. He found a girl's purse in the air conditioning/heating vent. It had her name and her money. We had learned not to put our entire night on hold trying to figure things out and everyone in the family having a miserable time, so we left for the dance. We talked on our way over to the dance and Michael kept denying all knowledge of the wallet. When we arrived at the dance the counselor could see we were upset and Eric asked for a private place to talk with Michael. They talked for awhile first about getting honest; and then once Michael admitted he stole the wallet, they talked about returning it and making amends. I really admired Eric's patience and care while trying to reach Michael.

We partied and danced until about 3:00AM and returned home. Theresa and Michael's friends were visiting from Houston. They were all at the dance and came back with us to spend the night at our house. We left them all in the living room and we went to bed. I guess I must have been very tired because I didn't wake up until the phone rang at 6:00AM. It was Theresa saying she was sorry to wake me but she didn't want us to get mad if we woke up and saw that they weren't downstairs or even in the house. Yes, I thought, I would definitely be mad if they were gone. She said that they were at their friend's house because they had to take off in a hurry last night. (Their friend's still owned their San Antonio house while they were temporarily living in Houston.) It seemed right after we went to bed a group of teens came over to get revenge on Michael for stealing things. They came to fight and apparently they were arguing in the street, fighting, and keying each others cars. One of the teens came in our house with a cigarette and Theresa had a hard time getting her to leave. My kids thought it best to just leave without telling us. They were thinking that we heard all the commotion and choose not to come downstairs. I asked why they would think that and they figured if we could hear Michael sneaking in through the back window or Theresa whispering on the phone in the middle of the night we surely heard the fighting. It was an interesting point. I was so tired, I knew to say

let's talk later. Another thing I learned is that I don't
have to make decisions right away, but definitely don't
put them off too long. We talked later and decided to
let go of this incident also.

XIX. More Therapy

I was seeing my therapist every week and sometimes Eric and I would see both our therapist together. All our issues were becoming enmeshed. There was a time that Eric and I would have the same discussion of things over and over again. I scheduled an appointment for all of us to get together and "talk" again so we could finally put an end to this same argument Eric and I would have over and over again. When we arrived, Eric's therapist asked who called this meeting. I said that I did. I told the therapist what my issue was with Eric. The therapist asked Eric to respond that issue. He said what he usually said back to me. The therapist stopped him and said "We'll talk about that issue later. First, deal with this issue." We both stopped and look at the therapist. We had been having this same argument over and over again and just realized we were talking about two different things. Sometimes an objective, safe third party can be so helpful.

One of the things that put a great wedge in Eric and my relationship was my deciding to go on a camping trip with some women friends to Oklahoma. It was the same week of our 25th Anniversary, June 1998. My desire for this trip was very strong and the desire for me not to go on this trip by Eric was also very strong. The hardship this event brought to our relationship was something that still causes friction. I don't regret going because I needed to do this and I believe if I didn't go I would have regrets.

I was under the impression I should call Eric every night while I was away like he did for me while he traveled. This became more and more painful for both of us and finally he said don't call every night. I pretended things were okay when they weren't. I'm not sure if I was doing a "fake it till you make" thing or not. But the pain was almost unbearable. To this day we don't talk about this trip.

I continued with therapy and just barely making it through each day. I was getting to a point that I didn't cry upon entering my therapist office, and at times I could actually talk. I was still having flashbacks and painful emotional feelings. I think when I was in emotional pain I just wanted to be left alone. I know today that this "push-away" as Eric called it hurt him a lot. I focused very little on Theresa and Michael or anything else. Every week the main focus was getting into therapy. It's how I survived.

We celebrated our 25th Anniversary out in Big Ben before I had gone on the trip with my friends. There was so much pain and resentment about the trip I would be going on that I think this celebration might have hurt us rather than helped. One night on the way home Eric stopped to take a picture of the sunset and I just panicked inside and became full of fear. I went back immediately to the night I was abused to just before I fell asleep as I watched the beautiful sunset. Even to write about this right now can stir those painful feelings.

Eric went to his therapist somewhat regularly. He read "Ghost in the Bedroom" and "Allies in Healing". Although he was really trying hard to be supportive he still seemed very clingy. In group he would share about being a "cling-on". (He's a Star Trek fan!) He said it cute and funny but in reality it was very difficult to live with.

I do admire him for sharing his truth though. Many people are afraid to get real about their marriages and share their ups and downs. Drug addiction will bring out every character defect you know and don't know. I believe that's why we work the twelve steps so that we can confront ourselves and our loved ones head on. If I have so much pain and uncertainty in myself, I certainly don't have any left over to give to a spouse. The program asks us to get a sponsor of the same sex. This is the same for addicts as well as family members. The only requirement for being a sponsor is to be working your own program, that is having a sponsor and actually doing the steps with them. This gives us an opportunity to really "talk" to someone who has walked this walk before us. They can be a guide as well as a sounding board. There is a saying that goes "A pain shared is halved, a joy shared is doubled." The more people we allow in our circle of trust the more we can grow.

XX. Theresa Graduates High School

For two years Theresa dated the same guy regularly. Many addicts after getting sober from drugs will switch addictions. For many people this addiction is sex and/or codependence. They say that drug addict/alcoholics don't get boyfriend/girlfriends – they take hostages. I had learned this early on in the program and then guess I had some relief that she had a relationship with another sober guy. So at least she wasn't sleeping with everyone like so many other drug addicts. There were times she wanted to stay out all night or come home early in the morning with a car full of friends. One night Eric made her drive all her friends home at 5:00 AM. He went with her to make sure she stayed awake.

In December 1998 graduation day came. Theresa and her boyfriend had broken up and she seemed a little lost. The actual graduation day seemed so anti-climatic. Theresa was not very excited and just Eric and I and a counselor from PDAP attended. She didn't want to go out to celebrate. She wanted pizza when we got home. It was sad for me and it looked sad for her. On another night we went out with some girls to Cracker Barrel – her choice of a restaurant.

I could see she was starting down that road toward using, BUDDing as we call it. It stands for Building Up to Drinking and Drugging. Withdrawing from conversations in the family and losing interest in any other activities were the main symptoms I could see. It was an accumulation of circumstances that made me realize that Theresa was using again and I knew I had to confront her.

Eric struggled believing there was anything seriously wrong and I remember him leading a meeting on being 100% sure before confronting. He admitted that he wanted to give the benefit of the doubt unless he was 100% sure but he realized this was a bad thing and a crutch for not confronting. Many people in the meeting agreed and would carry on as usual without that concrete evidence. The bottom line is to confront what you are seeing, as they say in recovery "if it walks like a duck, looks like a duck and quacks like a duck – it probably is a duck".

I found "not confronting" very frustrating and with a lot of prayer and thought I decided that I would not tolerate anything that looked like drug use again. My boundary was no drug use – period. In order to take care of myself I decided to leave home if I felt anyone was using drugs. I wouldn't leave for good but only until I knew my house was safe. I didn't share this with Eric or anyone else but I needed to assure myself that I didn't have to stay in the chaos if it was hurting too much. Theresa was doing the bare minimum again and there was an ache inside that made me know things were bad. Eric and I talked about the signs I was seeing and if there was a break in the boundary she'd have to go. I'm not sure what he was thinking but when the time came he was supportive.

XXI. Theresa Chooses to Leaves Home

Theresa had saved some money and we had just sold her the 1994 Saturn for $500.00. She would be working full time and we hoped this would help her self-esteem. The day after she bought the car I asked to borrow it real quick to run an errand. She said "sure". While I was out I needed a pen and many times there were pens in the glove compartment. I opened the glove box up and there were about 4 or 5 shot test tubes in there. I gave her a call and woke her up. I asked about the shot tubes and she said she found them on the Riverwalk. I felt so sad and with tears in my eyes I quietly said "Theresa, you're an alcoholic". "We'll talk tonight when dad and I come home." I knew that when an addicted person relapses they just don't use a little, they go right back to where they left off or worse. Later that evening when Eric came home I could hear him come in the front door. And then I heard Theresa talking. She was telling Eric good-bye. She would be going to live with the drug dealer. I was upstairs and I bent over the staircase and said "good-bye Theresa, I love you." "Bye mom, I love you too." That powerlessness, that almost hopelessness and the most depressing of all Theresa was choosing this. Choosing to go out and use drugs over living with a family that loved her. *When we talk about this now even Theresa will say when I chose to leave home rather than we "kicked her out".*

I imagined God wrapping His arms around me and telling me how sad He was too. I thought of Him telling me that He loved her more than me (hard for me to imagine) and that He couldn't do anything about this either. He gave her free will. I imagined Him sad and crying with me. He wanted the best for her too.

That is probably the most important lesson of my writing – this disease is so powerful that the drug addict will give up everything, including the most important people in their lives. And the concerned loved one, me, has to be the example and choose to allow this irrational decision, based in knowledge of the disease and the love of working the steps. I don't know another way to have recovery from the effects of mind-changing chemicals.

Last week a newcomer to the PDAP program asked me if anyone ever "lost" a child when the child was living out on the streets. After I thought awhile, I answered that the only children who I know died were still using and living at home. Later, however I did think of one adult child who

*died while she was out on her own. The overwhelming
majority, however, have never been "let go".*

During this time Eric wanted to have a relationship
with Theresa. I felt that I couldn't keep a relationship
while she was using. Once a week he would meet her
for coffee at Starbucks. All I asked was that he didn't
bring her home and also not give her money. Any
money would definitely go for drugs. I knew if I had
met with her I would not be able to follow through
on those boundaries because I could not stand to see
my daughter homeless or worse living with the dealer.
So every week they would meet and I would basically
pray for them and myself to just get through each
encounter.

I think by now Eric and I were sure we were both
committed to not only our marriage, but to our
relationship. We wanted more than something that
worked. We were seeking to be what God intended
each of us to be and to be that support for each other.
We would both do whatever it takes to look at ourselves
and to grow and share this with each other. We both
worked with our sponsors and therapists. Although
Theresa was gone we still tried to carry on with normal
family activities. Having fun and socializing is part
of a balanced life even though it is very difficult when
your child is living with the drug dealer and using
drugs and the other is showing more and more signs
of addiction.

XXII. Michael Meets Kim

It was June 19th 1999. It was day tubing on the river during the summer. This one was not quite as eventful for me as the last one. It was very pleasant and fun. I was driving Michael and some friends home, most of whom were girls. I really enjoyed these friends, especially one girl in particular. She seemed to bring out the best in Michael and for the first time he seemed to be carrying on a normal conversation with people. After the last of the kids were dropped off I said to Michael "Why don't you go out with a girl like that?" That girl turned out to be my future daughter-in-law.

Theresa was gone all summer, yet with Michael every day was somewhat chaotic. He would either want a car or need to be driven somewhere. One morning

Michael came downstairs while Eric and I were having breakfast. For Michael to be up this early, was highly unusual and a very bad sign. Michael said he wanted to talk to us before dad went to work.

"I was driving some friends home last night and in the rain I skid and hit a barbed wire fence. The Saturn did a three hundred sixty spin and all four sides hit the barbed wire fence. It's pretty much all scratched up and dented. I got one flat tire and the donut tire is on it right now."

Wow, I thought. "I guess everyone was alright?"

"Yeah" Michael said.

"Well, thanks for coming down here to tell us" Eric said.

Michael just stood there. There was silence. We looked at him and waited.

"There's more," Michael told us. "After that accident I didn't want to drive all the way out to Kim's on the small tire, so I came home and borrowed the station wagon."

"Okay", that was fine with us.

"But then", Michael said "I hit a deer but I don't think I killed him because I saw him run off. There's just a small dent in the front fender and the light fell out."

Two cars in one night. They were both drivable. We let it go as far as getting angry. We purchased "The Club" for each car. The consequences were that no one could drive the cars unless we gave specific permission and took "The Club "off.

I really couldn't stand the music Michael liked to work out to, so the rule was if I heard it and I didn't like it I would throw it away. At first this didn't bother Michael very much but then I could see anger starting to well up inside him. Since this was a change in his personality I was pretty certain drug use was involved.

The summer of 1999 seemed to have increasing tension. We had a lock on our bedroom door for years but now our college son, Chris, had one put on his door also. Both cars had "The Club" installed every night before we went to bed and as usual my purse or anything of value was always locked in our bedroom.

My recovery was so overwhelming for me. I lived to get free of the emotional pain, flashbacks and body memories. I was seeking answers. I decided to sign-up for LCDC course to get a drug abuse counseling license. I so much wanted to figure it out. How could a fine family like ours be going through so much turmoil? Michael was getting out of control, Theresa was out living with the drug dealer, our marriage became extremely shaky and my childhood abuse issues were controlling my days and nights. For years I didn't have a solid night's sleep. I had been going to therapy weekly for 3 years and I could feel relief yet it wasn't enough.

I sought answers that maybe someone knew. I would take a course and see where it leads.

I really knew that working the steps and being part of a support group was changing my life for the better when one night it was my turn to lead a Newcomers Meeting at PDAP. I was supposed to tell newcomers in the program about what PDAP did and how it helped in my life. Well, things were getting very difficult with Michael. I was pretty sure he was a cocaine addict and Theresa was out in the streets living with the drug dealer. How was I supposed to let new people know that this was a place of hope and miracles? Then I thought, look at myself. I am thinking of helping others feeling secure in God's love that everything will be alright. How can I not share that hope? Sometimes the worst of times can be used for the best of God.

As the summer moved on Michael seemed less interested in being with us and he was starting to have that same distant, withdrawn look Theresa used to have. *Every now and then I'd find some small baggies. These indicated Michael was selling, though I didn't know it at the time. Today many kids are doing methamphetamines so you may find broken light bulbs that kids use to cook their meth. The ingredients to make meth include fertilizer and over the counter cold medications. Also, for kids doing cocaine you might be missing spoons and razors. Spray paint or any aerosol can is an easy inhalant. It is wise to call a professional for help even in this early stage. Just using these products is deadly.*

One night, I had been waiting on the couch to confront Michael because it was well past curfew. He came home early in the morning. It had been a long while since I had to enforce the boundary of calling the police if he and/or the car were missing and I didn't do it this night. I asked him where he had been and I got the same old non responsive answer. I told him I was thinking he needed help like Theresa, that all the signs were there that he was using. He of all people should understand because of the pain he went through with us when Theresa was first getting help and we put her in treatment. Didn't he remember sharing with her on family week how much he wanted her to get better? I could see I was getting through to him.

Then he said "You should be worried about Theresa, not me. I bet you didn't even know she was pregnant."

He was certainly right about that. But I had really learned to stay focused when I was confronting someone. "Put it on the back burner Joanne" I said to myself.

"This isn't about Theresa," I said. "This is about you and what I see in you."

We continued talking about his behavior. And I took him for a drug test since he kept claiming he would pass one. Later after he slept we would talk more.

Later, when Michael was more coherent, I let him know that I would call the police and report him the next time he was out past curfew.

A few nights later this same scenario happened and rather than wait to confront and talk to Michael in the morning, I did call the police. Eric was home and the police officer arrived. The officer was trying to convince me not to press charges because Michael would have this offense on his record. I wasn't sure what to do and at this moment Michael walked in the house. He went up to his room and we didn't file charges.

XXIII. Drug Rehab 2

It was during this time that things seemed to be getting worse with Michael. He was spending all day sleeping and all night running around. He would be 18 in November and he would have to go out on his own if this behavior continued.

One afternoon a teacher called from school telling me about all the work Michael was missing in school and he was starting to fall asleep in class and he wasn't paying attention. I listened and prayed for the right words because I knew that I could do nothing for Michael to do better in school. I said "Have you said all this to him because I tell him to do those same things at home and maybe if he heard it from you too he would listen." There was silence on the other end of the line. I said

"Hello, are you there?" He said yes and he would talk to Michael. It gave me some relief.

In the state of Texas one of the worst nightmares for a parent with a child on drugs who is between the ages of 16 and 18 is that legally a parent is responsible for that child yet a parent cannot place their child in rehab against the child's will. Many parents whose children are in trouble with the law are held responsible for their child's behavior. This really lets the young person off the hook and puts an unreasonable burden on the parent. In my job as a PDAP family group counselor I have written letters to the courts to ask for parental support in giving responsibility and consequences back to the child.

In September Theresa called to ask if she could come home. She told us about her pregnancy and that she wanted to change. Wow I said I have to think about that and talk to dad because we can't have you living here like you did before. We made arrangements to talk later on the phone so I could tell her what she needed to do in order to come home and be part of our family again.

In our next conversation I explained that she had to do 7 things in order to live at home.

1. Go to 2 PDAP meetings/week, 1 PDAP counseling session/week, and 1 activity (Sign a release so I could check this out).
2. Get a fist (this means be one month sober)
3. Go to therapy

4. Get a job and pay rent of $100.00/month
5. Can't drive the car until sober 6 months
6. Clean up after herself in the house
7. Curfew 10:00PM on weekdays and Midnight on weekends

This was fine with her, although she wanted to come home right away. Part of me really hated to leave her out there knowing she was an easy target for getting hurt and also the high risk of using again but the part of me that knew about the disease knew she had to hurt and feel her consequences. She needed to know that home was not something she could ever take for granted again. I also knew that there were many people who knew and loved her because we were involved in a support group and they would help her if it came down to her being homeless.

Michael spent another night out and I knew I needed to call the police. I decided to offer him inpatient treatment rather than handling it legally. I spent one afternoon in October with Michael, sitting out back on our patio. At first he said there was no way he was using and I could drug test him. So we went to PDAP to get a form to have him drug tested. Then we came back and sat outside again. It was a warm, breezy, pleasant afternoon and it took all the presence of mind I could muster to talk about his disease and that I saw he needed to get more help. *There is a time when a person who is using drugs is in between being high and craving that he is able to be engaged in rational conversation. It doesn't happen often, but when it does you can use this window of opportunity to apply an intervention.* This was much easier on me emotionally this time because maybe the worst had happened already with Theresa. Michael seemed to hear some of what I was saying like there was a part of him that wanted help. I never really saw that with Theresa.

I told Michael all the symptoms I had seen in him and how they were worsening. He was staying out all night, getting in trouble at school with grades and tardiness; he looked tired and preoccupied all the time, like he was a zombie and I also told him that looking at him reminded me a lot of Theresa's symptoms. I could see the disease coming again. He listened without commenting much and then I left him to go to work. I gave Eric a call and I asked him to talk to Michael when he got home. Eric and I met quickly for dinner and I described the afternoon with Michael. Eric called PDAP and took Michael to talk to a counselor. The counselors gave Michael their best effort at reflecting his situation of using drugs and what the results were in destroying his life. Later that night, as Eric and Michael pulled up in the driveway, Michael admitted needing help. He said he would go to treatment. Michael asked if he could go over and say good-bye to his girlfriend, Kim. Eric waited for Michael to get packed, took him to say good-by to his girlfriend and arrived for treatment in the middle of the night.

The next day I withdrew Michael from school. As with Theresa you don't have to say why you are withdrawing your child so I didn't say anything in the main office. However, I did go to the teacher who had called me the month before and told him where Michael was going.

Michael was in a work study program and he had an early release and a job for credit. The teacher said he would talk to his employer about Michael returning after rehab.

The drug test came back clean although Michael knew it should have been positive for cocaine. This is one of the reasons I don't care for drug testing – too many false negatives. Sometimes it's better to confront all the issues or symptoms, because they show drug use and you can get results from that, however, sometimes drug tests are all we have to work with.

Theresa moved back home one week after Michael entered rehab. She had met all the requirements to live at home and I was cautiously optimistic again. She needed a job to pay her rent, which was only $100.00/ month. She also could not use our family car until she was sober 6 months. I took her over to the bus station to get a monthly pass and picked up some bus schedules so she could learn how to get around town. She was going to go for an interview and the closest bus stop to get her there was three miles away. I offered to drive her to the bus stop (not her job) so she could start managing her own life. I also offered to pick her up at the same place when she returned. I could see she was nervous but I was going to stand firm with not letting her use the car.

Later that day, during peak rush hour she called and said she was lost and had taken the wrong way to come home. She had gotten on the bus going the wrong way and she had absolutely no idea where she was. I told her to cross the street and get on the bus going back the way she had come. A little while later she called again. Right now she was at a gas station across the street from the bus stop.

My understanding was that she was at the bus stop across from where she interviewed. I said I would come to pick her up. I went to that bus stop. I drove there, rode around, went inside the gas station and called home. Chris said she called looking for me. After another search I called home again and exchanged more details. She was at the gas station across the street from the bus stop I had dropped her off at in the morning. We had a good laugh. But also Theresa said how much she appreciated driving. Since that experience every bus stop we would pass she commented on how hard it was to wait in the hot sun for the bus.

She ended up getting a job at Starbucks where Eric could bring her to work most mornings or I could bring her later in the day. We'd also share picking her up from work also. The bus thing didn't work out but she still had to be sober for 6 months before she drove again.

I wasn't sure she'd stick to all the rules but I was sure I would stick to all the consequences. There would be no more disease in my house.

During family week Chris and Theresa came up for the counseling and family sharing day. It was beneficial because Michael got to see that everyone was on the same page and we all saw the same symptoms in him and that he was getting worse. He seemed moderately convinced.

On the last night of family week he was allowed to go out on pass. Eric and I took him to Cracker Barrel, one of his favorite restaurants. He had a beef stew dinner as his appetizer and a regular meal for his dinner. We still laugh about that today. He really seemed to appreciate a good meal.

Later that evening the three of us went up to the cabin that Eric and I were renting and took a boat out on the river. The sun was beginning to set and it was warm, calm and beautiful. You could see the orange sun reflecting off the water for a long way. We made small talk and I realized how little time we ever really got to spend alone with Michael. I wondered what if this was the best it ever got with him. What if, after rehab, he went back to doing the same old thing? What if this evening was last sober day we had with him? I cherished that evening. And inside I changed. I understood that living in the present I would have a wonderful memory of today but fearing the future would rob me of that time.

The next day we were getting ready to leave the treatment facility. Eric and I decided to take a walk up Serenity Hill again just as we did 3 years earlier when Theresa was there. On our last visit to the see the beautiful view we separated and became somewhat depressed because of all the horrible events people placed on their rocks. One of the exercises they do at rehab is to think about the burdens they carry and write them on a rock and leave the rock on Serenity Hill as symbol for leaving their burdens with their Higher Power. On that first visit, I became so overwhelmed with grief for the pain Theresa must have felt in order to leave one of those rocks. On this second trip up the hill I started to feel joy that there was a place for people to leave their burdens so they didn't have to take them home. I had a change of heart in how I looked at the world.

I learned later that his girlfriend, who we were bringing with us on Sunday visitation, was bringing drugs for Michael. Michael used and sold drugs in rehab. He also used the Freon in the facility's air-conditioner unit.

Michael came home and had his eighteenth birthday. He was a senior in high school and he needed his job in order to graduate. He was afraid about whether or not he would get his old job back. He asked me to take him to some new places to apply for work so he wouldn't have to face his old employer. He applied at several places as if this were his first job and then said he'd give it a try at the old place. He went to ask for his old job back and was totally honest with the people there. They were very receptive and had wanted to give him another chance. He seemed so happy. *This situation was relief because I tried to convince Michael that honesty was the best policy, not to offer more than was asked but when asked to tell the truth. Later as he "worked the steps" he would "make amends" to all those people he had harmed.* I still was not convinced that Michael was staying clean and sober, but I had definite boundaries and no tolerance for drugs. *This feeling of uncertainty*

Joanne D.

whether to believe he was staying sober or not, stays for quite awhile after the user gets sober. Relapse is a part of recovery, so my part in this is confronting the wrong doing and enforcing my boundaries.

XXIV. New Years Eve 1999

The next month, on New Years Eve, Michael and Kim decided to join us for the mid-night meeting. New Years Eve is so much fun in PDAP. We spend the entire night out on the town – going to movies, bowling, playing laser tag and then a mid-night meeting and breakfast out. Michael and Kim looked bad. My heart ached. Would this problem ever end? Since he wasn't breaking any rules we would be drug testing again and with the next positive he'd have to leave. I let go for the evening and enjoyed the rest of the night as best I could.

What happened next was a miracle that only God could have planned. Michael and Kim got clean and sober together. Michael admitted his drug use and started working a program. He got a sponsor and started working the steps. He started doing better in school and going to meetings and being somewhat responsible at home. That New Year's Eve is still his and Kim's sobriety date. I believe the seeds were planted all along in PDAP and in rehab for Michael.

William and his fiancée, Nancy, came out to visit in March. Theresa had another month before the baby was due. We rented a cabin on the Frio River for anyone in the family who wanted to go with us. It was very relaxing and fun. Theresa slept the entire time we were there and then the day after we got back, her water broke. She went into the hospital and the next day, Saturday. William and Nancy left. Then, on Sunday, we went to visit. And on Monday morning Theresa called "Mom, can you come in to the hospital? I think I'm having the baby." "Okay", I replied thinking since labor just started I'd have a long time. When I arrived an hour later she was ready to be wheeled to the delivery room. "Please come in with me mom." Then the baby's father handed me a camera and asked me to take pictures. I did my best.

Charlie was born later that morning. He was less than five pounds and went into the Intensive Care Unit. Other than being born a month early and small, all was well. Theresa came home and rotated between the dad's house and her own. She got worn out but I let her do whatever she thought was important for herself and the baby.

At this time I had just started working my practicum at an intensive outpatient facility. I had to obtain hours for my license. Michael had been sober for several months and I began to let him take the car to his after school job. Sometimes, he would drop me off first and I would watch him drive away. I was going in to counsel parolees and probationers and I thought of how I would want someone to talk to Michael if he were a client here. In fact someday, I thought, Michael may be one of these clients. I decided then that I would always treat people like they were my family and be open and honest while always maintaining my boundaries.

Well, Michael's graduation day came in May. Eric and I were not quite sure he would really graduate because he liked to wait until the last minute to tell us any facts or changes, especially if they were negative. Eric and I commented to each other that he had his cap and gown. We had a family dinner and cake to celebrate. When we went over to the Coliseum and his name was in the brochure, we commented that possibly there would still be some kind of delay in his graduating. They called his name. He walked the stage and graduated. The diploma was real and valid. Wow. After graduation, the store Michael was working for early school release, hired him full time.

Since we had sold our house in Maryland and finished paying for Rehab with our equity, we decided to buy our own home instead of renting. Theresa was planning on marrying Charlie's dad and moving out, Michael always talked about moving out of our house, he said he couldn't wait, and Chris said as soon as college was over he'd be gone.

In June, the first change in plans came as Theresa and I were planning the wedding. We had all the arrangements made and she put the invitations in the mailbox out front. I got a call at work that said "Mom, I don't know if I'm doing the right thing." "Go get the invitations right away. You can have some time to think today. We'll talk tonight." She decided that she couldn't go through with marriage. It was okay for her to live with us as long as she needed. She had been sober almost a year now and trust was coming back into our relationship.

We were unable to get the money back for the reception at the Officers Club because it was less than month before the Wedding date. I called PDAP and asked about having a fund raiser since we had to pay for the food and hall anyway. Since Theresa wouldn't be having a Wedding she asked if she could tell her story and volunteered to speak about her experience, strength and hope after dinner. It was a night I will never forget because I saw another miracle. In her speech, she talked about what good parents we were. That meant so much more to me than almost anything because it was always so hard to believe I didn't do something wrong.

A month later we found a house that was perfect for us and since Theresa and Charlie would be moving in with us there would be plenty of room. And if anyone else needed a little time before moving out it would be okay. It was going to take some time because it was still being built. Chris, Michael, Theresa and Charlie along with Eric and me moved into our new home in September 2000.

Then, in October 2000, came the next change in plans. Kim was pregnant.

She did not want to live in her home anymore. She was only seventeen. She had another year of high school to finish. I would not allow them to live together in my house unless they were married. I know this was old-fashioned but it was a boundary for me. The ball was in their court depending on what they wanted to do. Michael continued to work full time for the store that hired him back and there was trust coming back there too. Then Michael and Kim were married just before Thanksgiving and Kim moved in with our family. There were 7 of us living under one roof until Joseph was born in June and then we were one big family of 8.

At this point we had known so much worse chaos that our biggest problem was cooking after 9:00 pm. Michael and Kim were the first to move out after Christmas 2001. Theresa found a place with a friend in Jan 2002 and Chris was building a house which would be ready in March 2002.

XXV. The Present

That brings my story of drug addiction in our family full circle because the house is so quiet now, except on Sundays when the family gathers at our house. Chris is leading us in a bible study in the evenings and all of us are sharing our spiritual growth. Eric and I have a really solid, loving, intimate relationship that we would have never known if we hadn't gone through the experiences we had. We are each on our own spiritual path and attend different churches for right now.

I thank God for every day that I am not in emotional pain and that I am alive to follow His will for me.

Sometimes I still struggle with the reality of the sexual abuse that happened as a child. I'm not always sure it really happened but I am sure of the PTSD and the flashbacks.

I accept the reality of experiencing that trauma as a child while I was an adult. Sometimes I struggle with thinking I had a nervous breakdown while I was in recovery. Whatever the truth is I know I kept walking day after day and I was able to grow in faith.

As far as finding the answers to all those questions about how this could happen to a family like ours – It just happens, no one is immune. There is no cause, no control and no cure for the disease of addiction. I try to convey this to parents at my job. I am a counselor at PDAP for the Family Group and the New Generations Group. The Family Group is for parents and spouses or other relatives and friends of drug addicts. The New Generation group is for kids who don't use drugs but are being affected by someone who is using, usually a brother, sister or parent. There is at least one yearly retreat for each of these groups.

Just last year we had our New Generations retreat at the same place I had gone on my first retreat.

It was a great retreat and the kids all got together to make a surprise for me. Under the walk bridge there are a lot of rocks. The kids placed rocks together to write out PDAP and JD, my initials. Then all day they wanted to show me their surprise. At dinner time we all walked over the bridge to the restaurant and they stood below the bridge and they yelled up to me "Joanne, look what we made you." Their parents and I stood there and waved and said "It looks great." Eight years earlier I was ready to jump off that very same bridge and today five kids were thanking me. I got tears in my eyes thinking about what God can do with a life if you listen.

121

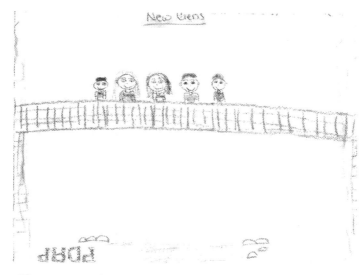

This is a copy of a picture the New Gens kids drew for me after the retreat.
I have had it hanging in my office to remind me of what God can do with an open heart.

Recently someone asked me about what my job was. I told him a little bit about what I do and he said "Well, I think it's all the parents' fault. The responsibility lies with them." I told him that wasn't true because there are so many nice parents whose children are addicted to drugs. I wanted to tell him more about my story but he quickly changed the subject to something less controversial. It really prompted me to complete my story along with something the pastor said last Sunday. He said that over 17,000 accidental deaths occur each year in the US as a direct result of alcohol. That statistic does not include deaths from drugs or indirect deaths from alcohol. If nothing else comes from this book I hope that every parent of a teenager realizes that **any** alcohol or drug use is abuse and can lead to addiction – no matter how good a person or family you are. And if a loved one should become addicted there is so much hope of not only getting well, but of a happy productive life for all. In my case, I am grateful to be healthier and happier than I was before the illness of addiction affected my family.

The Twelve Steps of PDAP

1. We admitted that mind-changing chemicals had caused at least part of our lives to become unmanageable.

2. We found it necessary to stick with winners in order to grow.

3. We realized that a Higher Power, expressed through our love for each other, could help restore us to sanity.

4. We made a decision to turn our will and our lives over to the care of God, as we understand Him.

5. We made a searching and fearless moral inventory of ourselves.

6. We admitted to God, to ourselves, and another human being the exact nature of our wrongs.

7. We became willing to allow our Higher Power, through the love of the group, to help change our way of life and humbly asked Him to help us change.

8. We made a list of all persons we had harmed and became willing to make amends to them all.

9. We made direct amends to such people, whenever possible, except when to do so would injure them, others or ourselves.

10. We continue to look at ourselves and when wrong promptly admit it.

11. We have sought through prayer and meditation to improve our conscious contact with our Higher Power; we have chosen to call God, praying only for knowledge of His will for us and the courage to carry that out.

12. We, having had a spiritual awakening as a result of these steps, try to carry our love and understanding to others and practice these principles in our daily lives.

The Promises

The Promises are the guaranteed results of working the 12 Steps thoroughly and honestly.

1. If we are painstaking about this phase of our development, we will be amazed before we are halfway through.

2. We will know a new freedom and a new happiness.

3. We will not regret the past nor wish to shut the door on it.

4. We will comprehend the word serenity, and we will know peace.

5. No matter how far down the scale we have gone, we will see how our experience can benefit others.

6. That feeling of uselessness and self-pity will disappear.

7. We will lose interest in selfish things and gain interest in our fellows.

8. Self-seeking will slip away.

9. Our whole attitude and outlook on life will change.

10. Fear of people and of economic insecurity will leave us.

11. We will intuitively know how to handle situations which used to baffle us.

12. We will suddenly realize that God is doing for us what we could not do for ourselves.

I would like to say a special thank you to my parents for their compassion and understanding, my brothers and sisters who I love so much, my husband and children who allowed so much of themselves to be disclosed to help others and to my fellow recovery travelers who help me grow.

Also a special thank you to all the PDAP supporters who have invested so much time, money and meeting/office space in order to help families, like mine, overcome the effects of mind changing chemicals.

Thank you to the board members and the administrative office for making it possible to work in financial security. Thank you to House of Prayer Lutheran Church, Christ Episcopal Church, and Church of the Holy Cross Episcopal Church for allowing PDAP - San Antonio, to operate out of your facilities. Sharing your home with drug addicts and their families is a reflection of what God wants us all to do.

And a special thank you to all the PDAP counselors who help change not only many young people's lives, but their families' lives as well. I truly have a new normal now as I try to pass on what was given to me.

If you need assistance or would like to make a donation please call the Palmer Drug Abuse Program- San Antonio at 210-227-2634.

CPSIA information can be obtained at www.ICGtesting.com
Printed in the USA
LVOW070859030512

280049LV00002B/1/A